STEAMPUNK
softies

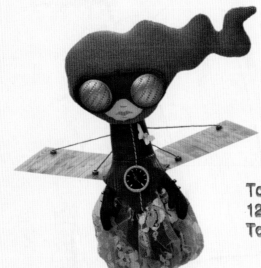

SCIENTIFICALLY MINDED DOLLS
FROM A PAST THAT NEVER WAS

Sarah Skeate &
Nicola Tedman

Andrews McMeel
Publishing, LLC
Kansas City • Sydney • London

ISBN: 978-1-4494-0600-4

Library of Congress Control Number: 2010940191

This book was conceived, designed, and produced by
Ivy Press
210 High Street
Lewes
East Sussex BN7 2NS
United Kingdom
www.ivy-group.co.uk

Creative Director: Peter Bridgewater
Publisher: Jason Hook
Conceived by: Sophie Collins
Editorial Director: Tom Kitch
Senior Designer/Photographer: James Lawrence
Designer: Tonwen Jones
Illustrator: Sarah Skeate

Printed in China

Color origination by Ivy Press Reprographics

11 12 13 14 15 IYP 12 11 10 9 8 7 6 5 4 3 2 1

The steam engine "Rhoda" used on pages 2 and 57 appears in memory of Alf Funnell.

IMPORTANT!
Safety warning: The figures are not toys. Many have small, removable parts and should be kept out of the reach of small children.

CONTENTS

INTRODUCTION

The steampunk movement is invading the craft world, and steampunk softies are the very embodiment of steampunk values. Eccentric, individual, and very appealing, steampunk softies may be plushy in the middle, but their exteriors are all business. Each has his or her part to play in the past-that-never-was that is the essence of steampunk, and we've given a hint of backstory in the characters' individual introductions. Whether you choose to start with Tompion Zeitgeist, the illusionist, with his floating magic globe and hypnotic revolving eyes; Charity Storm, the aviatrix, with her built-in wings and glamour-girl hair; or Floyd Fastknight, the explorer, with his charts, maps, and pennant, you'll be creating a strong character with an astonishing amount of personality for someone less than six inches high.

Read through all the instructions for your chosen project before you start—steampunk softies aren't challenging in their construction, but they are detailed, and the ones toward the back of the book are quite complex. Then line up your materials, clear a work surface, and get ready for some truly enjoyable and creative crafting!

BEFORE YOU START

All eight steampunk personalities have a wide variety of hardware detailing to help them get in character, and you're sure to enjoy the construction as well as the sewing aspects of making them. Read these pointers before you start, though; you'll find them invaluable as you work your way through the projects.

STEAMPUNK MATERIALS AND ACCESSORIES

All the softies have long and detailed lists of materials. Don't be frightened off by this: the vast majority of these are available in most large craft stores (or online from good craft materials' suppliers), and a surprising number of the more esoteric looking details are made from jewelry findings—also obtained from craft and beading stores. A very few materials, though, are vintage or have slightly more unusual origins. If you're the sort of person (and most steampunk enthusiasts are) who keeps drawers and boxes of old remnants—keys, buttons, the knob that fell off that old clock you were so fond of—look through your treasures and improvise with something individual that looks right with the character you're making. Don't feel you have to copy every element slavishly—these softies are intended to be unique to their maker; try out different colors, finishes, or details. You'll love the results.

CUTTING OUT

Most printed patterns show a dotted internal line and a solid exterior line—you cut along the exterior (cutting) line and sew along the internal line—and the space between is the seam allowance. You'll find that the steampunk patterns are slightly different. They have only a solid line, and this is the line you will be sewing along. The step-by-step instructions given for each character will tell you how much seam allowance to leave around the pieces before you cut them out. The reason for this is that the softies use a lot of different materials, from sheet acetate to leather and suede, and the pieces are often sewn before they are actually cut out of the piece of material, so it makes more sense to treat patterns and materials individually, according to the steampunk and its particular make up.

GLUING

There's just as much gluing as there is sewing in these projects, so check out the different types of glue before you start, and be sure to use the right kind for each application: many of the softies' pieces are very small and whether they're fabric, leather, plastic, or metal, they need to be stuck securely to get a successful end result. The glues you'll need are specified in the materials lists and the steps, but to clear up any confusion, here's a description of the main types:

Latex adhesive Mostly used on porous fabrics. Spread a thin layer on both of the surfaces to be stuck together, leave to dry for a minute or two, then align the surfaces and press together.

Contact adhesive Used in exactly the same way as latex adhesive, this solvent-based glue bonds a much wider range of surfaces together.

Superglue This is the toughest glue type and it sticks together almost anything; but it acts instantly, so you need to be accurate and fast when using it.

Epoxy glue Usually comes in two tubes. Mix a little of the contents of each together. Sets very hard and will bond most things together, but most brands take a little time to dry, so you may need to support elements while the glue sets.

PVA glue Water-soluble glue that can be mixed with acrylic to make a "paint" that covers plastic.

Glue stick Stick of solid glue; good for sticking paper to paper or other surfaces that need only a small amount of adhesion.

SEWING LINE

AGING

Your softies will look much more authentically steampunk with some judicious aging applied—and it's easily done with very few props. This section shows a wide range of simple ways to make your materials look as though they've lived longer and harder lives. Brand-new fabrics from your local fabric shop will acquire a vintage patina in minutes.

AGING WITH WAX

MATERIALS AND EQUIPMENT
- Fabric or leather to be distressed
- Plain candle
- Parchment paper
- Electric iron
- Scissors

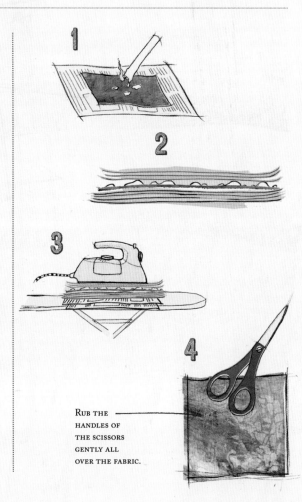

1 / Lay the fabric down on a protected surface (a few layers of newspaper will do), light the candle, and drip wax, drop by drop, over the whole area you want to age.

2 / Cut six pieces of parchment paper, each the same size or slightly larger than your fabric piece. Sandwich the waxed fabric between the paper, three layers on top and three underneath.

3 / Heat the iron to medium heat, lay plenty of newspaper on your ironing board, put the fabric/paper sandwich on top, and iron firmly but quickly over all the layers so that the wax melts (any overspill will be caught by the parchment paper). Go over the layers with the iron several times. Leave to cool.

4 / Peel the paper off the fabric sandwich. Bend and fold the fabric with your hands to crack the wax. Finally, rub the surface down with the smooth handles of a pair of scissors—this will give your fabric a truly aged looking patina and texture.

RUB THE HANDLES OF THE SCISSORS GENTLY ALL OVER THE FABRIC.

TIMEWORN FABRICS

TOOTHPASTE (1)

This makes a very effective spot-stain for areas that you want to look particularly worn. It works best on thick, dark fabrics. Simply squeeze a tiny amount of white toothpaste directly onto your fabric (a spot not larger than a peppercorn to start with), rub well in with your fingers, then rinse the fabric and leave to dry. Result: material that appears whitened with age and wear!

CHALK (2)

Chalk dirties fabrics very effectively, but it works best on materials with some texture. For the subtlest effect, choose two chalk crayons, each one shade off the fabric you're aging. Rub the paler one lightly over the fabric first, then smudge it with your fingers. Repeat with the darker crayon. Work the chalk into the fabric gently but thoroughly; if it isn't rubbed in, it will rub off on anyone who touches your softie.

SCRATCHING (3)

This works best on leather to give the look of heavy use. Use a sharp point (A bradawl works best, but one blade of a pair of sharp scissors will do.) to make a series of crisscross scratches over the surface. Don't go too deep, just enough to penetrate the surface of the leather. To get an authentically aged look, rub some chalk or a very little soil into the scratches with your fingers, then wipe the leather with a damp cloth.

BLEACHING (4)

This technique is good for felt that looks too fresh and new. Fill a glass bowl with water to a depth of about four inches (ten centimeters). Add a tablespoon of bleach, using a stainless-steel spoon, as bleach will corrode silver or plastic. Add your fabric, stir well, and leave for a couple of hours. Rinse the fabric in clean water and leave to dry. This proportion will give a subtle effect. If you want something more dramatic you can add more bleach, but don't overdo it or you will weaken your fabric.

TOMPION ZEITGEIST

MATERIALS & EQUIPMENT

- Medium-weight gray wool fabric, 12 in./30 cm square
- White felt, 2¾ x 4 in./7 x 10 cm
- Pale gray suede, 4 x 4 in./10 x 10 cm
- Gray felt, 2¾ x 4¾ in./7 x 12 cm
- Sewing thread in dark gray, white, and pale gray
- Embroidery floss in dark gray
- Opaque white playing marble with swirl pattern, ¾ in./2 cm diameter
- Brass tube, 2 in./5 cm length, ⅛ in./6 mm diameter (If you don't have an odd piece at home, ask a hardware store to cut to length.)
- Dressmaking pins to hold cards
- 2 cogwheels (Our examples measure 1 in./2.5 cm diameter and ⅝ in./15 mm diameter, but use what you can find—other sizes will work.)
- Pack of miniature playing cards (from novelty, craft, or toy store)
- Flat, small charm to act as Tompion's pendant
- 8 pipe cleaners
- Packet of small plastic toy-filling pellets
- Small quantity of soft toy stuffing
- Sheet of acetate, letter size
- Double-sided tape
- Low-tack masking tape
- Epoxy glue
- Superglue
- PVA glue
- Glue stick
- Contact adhesive
- Latex adhesive
- Gold acrylic paint
- Small piece of rough sandpaper
- Small plastic food container
- Pale fabric pencil
- Disappearing marking pen
- Dark gray chalk pastel
- Sharp scissors
- Sewing needle
- Pair of tin snips
- Knitting needle

Note: Tompion is made with a mixture of hand and machine sewing.

Whether you find Tompion intriguing or sinister is very much up to you. People talk about him behind his back and the things they say are sometimes disquieting. Is he a harmless trickster or a conscienceless fraud? He's said to have invented a teleporter, an infernal machine that runs on the little-known mineral hypnosium. Is it true, or is it just another of his tricks and illusions? Only Tompion knows. Don't hold his gaze for too long…

EYES AND BROWS ARE A SINGLE UNIT—A SHEET OF THIN ACETATE WITH A LITTLE EMBROIDERED SATIN STITCH.

THE ELABORATE "WHEEL OF FORTUNE" UNDER THE EDGE OF THE GOWN IS SIMPLY CONSTRUCTED FROM TWO SMALL COGWHEELS, SOME MINIATURE PLAYING CARDS, AND FOUR DRESSMAKING PINS.

THE "SUSPENDED" GLOBE IS HELD ALOFT WITH A TINY PIECE OF TUBING GLUED THROUGH THE FRONT OF TOMPION'S GOWN.

THE HANDS ARE MADE FLEXIBLE BY MEANS OF PIPE CLEANERS INSERTED INSIDE THE WHITE GLOVES.

TOMPION ZEITGEIST STANDS 8½ IN./ 21.5 CM TALL.

TO MAKE TOMPION ZEITGEIST

1 / Photocopy, or scan and print, the pattern pieces from page 73 and cut them out.

TO MAKE THE CARDS AND THE GLOBE

2 / Rub a small patch of the glaze off the marble using the sandpaper. Turn the plastic food container upside down and stick the marble in a corner of the base, rough patch up, using double-sided tape. Mix a small quantity of epoxy glue, dab it on one end of the tube, and stick the tube to the roughened part of the marble. Use tape to secure the tube to the inside of the container to hold it until the glue has dried.

3 / Snip the heads off four dressmaking pins using tin snips. Lay the larger of the two cogwheels face down and use superglue to stick the pins in position—imagine a clock face and stick one at 11 o'clock and one at 5 o'clock, then space the other two evenly between them. Turn over, and stick the smaller cogwheel partially overlapping the larger at 12 o'clock. Leave to dry. Mix the acrylic paint with a drop of PVA glue and paint the cogwheels and pins gold.

4 / Position four mini playing cards over the pins and stick together with a glue stick at the points where the corners overlap. Use masking tape to stick the cards in position on the front of the cogwheels, then turn over and spread epoxy glue along each pin where it touches the back of each card. When dry, spread a thin layer of contact adhesive on each card, and then spread contact adhesive on the picture side of another four cards. When dry, stick the pairs of cards together, sandwiching the pins between them.

TO MAKE THE BODY, SLEEVES, AND GLOVES

5 / Fold the wool fabric right sides in and place the robe pattern piece with its edge along the fold. Draw around the hole marked on the robe front, too. Cut the robe out, then draw around the body plug and the body base on the remaining fabric and cut out. Draw a line on the robe with a fabric pencil along the dotted line on the pattern piece.

6 / Bring the far edge of the robe piece over to the marked line, thread a needle with dark gray thread, and hand sew the edge along the line using a whipstitch. Don't pass the thread all the way through the fabric so the seam is invisible on the outside.

7 / Pin the body base to the robe bottom and sew it in place using dark gray thread and a small overstitch. Stand the body up and fill it with plastic pellets 1¼ in./3 cm from the open top. Fill the remaining gap with soft toy stuffing.

8 / When the body is fully stuffed, pin the piece for the body plug in place, lining up the points marked B, and sew using dark gray thread and a small overstitch.

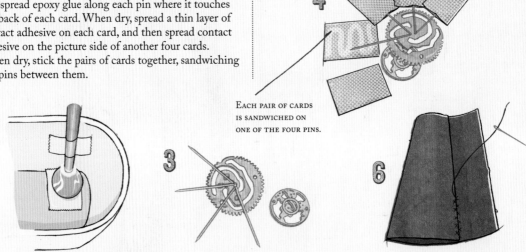

EACH PAIR OF CARDS
IS SANDWICHED ON
ONE OF THE FOUR PINS.

9 / Place the sleeve patterns on the wrong side of the wool, draw around them, and cut them out. Cut out the diamond shape marked on the left sleeve. Use dark gray thread and a baseball stitch (see illustration) to sew up the diamond shape (this creates the angle in the left arm).

10 / Butt the long sides of each sleeve together and pin. Start at the cuff end of each sleeve and use dark gray thread to sew them together with a baseball stitch.

11 / Cut the white felt into two equal rectangles and sandwich them together. Check that the lines between the fingers are cut to their ends on the glove pattern, then place it face up on one end of the felt and draw around it with a disappearing marking pen. Turn the pattern piece over and draw around it at the other end of the felt. Thread the sewing machine with white thread and sew around the gloves (without cutting them out), leaving the wrist ends open. Sew right down between each finger, turn round and sew back over your stitching and around the next finger. Turning the sewing machine wheel by hand will give you more control.

12 / Cut the gloves out as close to the stitching as possible, but do not cut out the individual fingers. Push a pipe cleaner into the thumb and each finger through the open ends, and push a few wisps of soft toy stuffing into the palm and back of each glove. Thread a needle with white thread and stitch the open ends of the gloves closed, sewing between the pipe cleaners.

13 / With one glove, twist the pipe cleaners together to form a single "arm," then fold them over toward the glove, measuring as you go. The overall length from tip of glove to end of pipe cleaner arm should be 4 in./10 cm. Repeat with the second glove and the other pipe cleaners. Bind both pipe cleaner arms with white thread, winding it around and knotting it firmly.

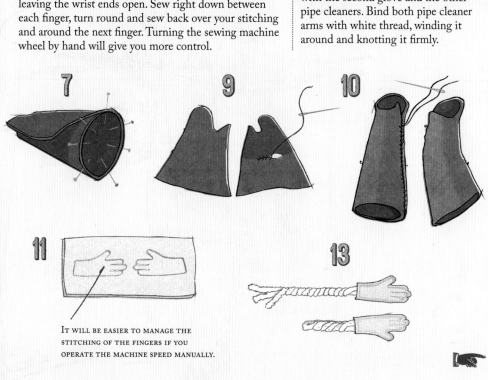

IT WILL BE EASIER TO MANAGE THE STITCHING OF THE FINGERS IF YOU OPERATE THE MACHINE SPEED MANUALLY.

14 / Push the end of the left arm up inside the left sleeve. Hold it against the body and pin in place on the body's left side (refer to the photograph for the position). Fold the top end of the sleeve back and stitch the pipe-cleaner arm in place. Pull the sleeve back over the shoulder and stitch the top of the sleeve in place using a small overstitch. Repeat with the right arm.

15 / Use a knitting needle to push a small amount of soft toy stuffing up into the shoulders to fill them out a little. Bend the left arm into position, using the photograph of the finished figure as a guide.

TO MAKE THE HEAD

16 / Draw around the head pattern on the gray suede and cut out leaving a ¼ in./6 mm seam allowance around it. Thread the sewing machine with pale gray thread and sew the two long sides together. Cut the bottom edge off along the line and turn the head right side out.

17 / Press the head flat with the center seam at the back (open the seam allowance inside with your fingers). Lay the head pattern on top of the suede, centering it, and draw the shape of the top of the head on the front with a disappearing marking pen. Sew the top of the head closed

with pale gray thread, cut off the seam allowance, and fill with soft toy stuffing through the open base. Sew the head onto the top of the body using a small overstitch.

18 / Draw around the shirt collar pattern on the white felt with a disappearing marking pen and cut it out. Place it in front of the base of the head and draw around it, then cover the back of the collar and the marked area with latex adhesive, leave to dry for a minute, then press the collar in place.

19 / Draw around the robe collar pattern on the wool fabric and cut it out, then place it around the base of the head with the gap in front. Mark the position, cover the back of the robe collar and the area marked on the head with latex adhesive, leave to dry for a minute, then stick the robe collar in place.

20 / Fold the gray felt in half and lay the hair pattern on top of it. Draw around the pattern using a disappearing marking pen, and machine stitch over the line with pale gray thread, leaving a ⅜ in./1 cm gap at the lower end. Stuff with soft toy stuffing, hand sew the opening closed, and cut the hair shape out as close to the stitching as possible.

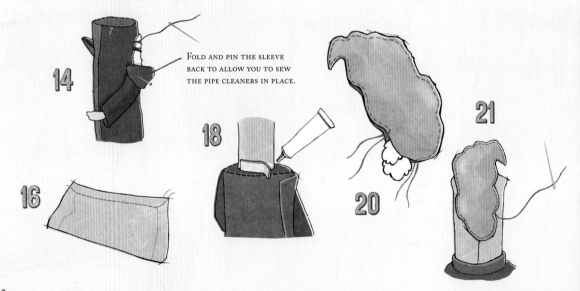

FOLD AND PIN THE SLEEVE BACK TO ALLOW YOU TO SEW THE PIPE CLEANERS IN PLACE.

21 / Use pale gray thread to stitch the hair to the back of the head, leaving ⅝ in./16 mm sticking up above the top of the head and catching the suede with small stitches.

22 / Draw two shaded semicircles on the face with the dark gray chalk pastel. Blend them slightly with your fingers.

23 / Photocopy the eyebrows and eyes onto the acetate and cut them out, leaving about ¾ in./2 cm margin all around them so that you have a rectangle of acetate. Thread a fine sewing needle with three strands of the dark gray embroidery floss and sew over the eyebrow shapes, working from the center to the eyebrow's end and stitching across the brow from top to bottom edge. Leave a long tail at the beginning (rather than tying a knot; work it in as you go) and don't place the stitches too close together or you will make a long hole in the acetate. Practice on a spare piece of acetate before you begin. When you get to the curly end of a brow, finish the thread off by passing it carefully under your stitches and trimming it.

24 / Cut the eyebrow and eye unit, leaving a tiny margin around the stitching.

TO FINISH THE FIGURE

25 / Cut out the hole in the front coat flap, mark through the hole onto the body with a pale fabric pencil, and cut a hole in the body also. Push the rod with the marble on the end into the body through both holes. Pin the cogwheel-and-card unit in position under the coat flap, then pin the pendant charm on the chest, just under the collar. Remove the rod with the marble from the body and use dark gray thread to sew the pendant and the cogwheel-and-card unit in place. Sew a line of tiny catching stitches from below the hole in the coat front down to the coat edge and under the coat flap to hold the coat in place.

26 / Push the rod with the marble back into the body through the cut holes and secure it with a few drops of superglue around the rod where it enters the body. Leave to dry, propped up.

27 / Thread a needle with a single strand of dark gray embroidery floss and sew the acetate piece in place on the head, stitching carefully through the brow using existing holes from the eyebrow stitches. Be very careful not to tear or slit the acetate and finish the thread off inside the head.

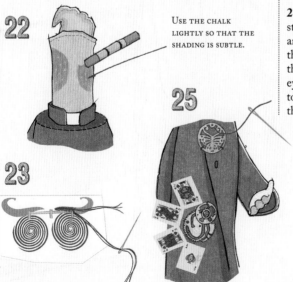

USE THE CHALK LIGHTLY SO THAT THE SHADING IS SUBTLE.

FATHOMLESS TILT

MATERIALS & EQUIPMENT

- Piece or pieces of thin pale gray suede, approximately 12 in./30 cm square. (You may have to buy several smaller pieces, as suede comes in skins or parts-skins, rather than by length.)
- Piece of thin brown leather, approximately 6 in./ 15 cm square, for the helmet rim and the belt
- Piece of white cotton, approximately 6 x 3 in./ 15 x 7.5 cm
- Buttonhole thread in yellow, gray, and beige
- Sewing thread in gray
- Small buckle, about $\frac{1}{2}$ in./12 mm wide. This could be new or taken from an old watchstrap.
- 6 stainless-steel buttonhead screws, with nuts, $\frac{1}{2}$ in./12 mm long
- 2 clock keys—you may find these at the back of a drawer or in a junk store. They can be mismatched, but should be approximately 2 in./5 cm long.
- Small quantity of soft toy stuffing
- Packet of plastic toy-filling pellets in the smallest size available
- Small piece of thin cardstock, approximately 4 in./ 10 cm square
- Small piece of paper
- Small clear plastic food container lid, approximately 4 in./10 cm diameter
- Empty plastic milk carton
- Plain white candle
- Fabric pencil
- Felt-tip pens in black and pink
- Latex adhesive
- Glue stick
- Contact adhesive
- Sharp scissors
- Sewing and embroidery needles
- Bradawl
- Hole punch
- Allen wrench to fit buttonhead screws
- Pair of needle-nosed pliers

Note: Parts of Fathomless will be easier to make with a sewing machine. If you are using a machine, use a regular, not leather, sewing needle—it will be able to cope with the very thin leather or suede.

He isn't human, that's for sure; despite his sonorous name, no one's quite sure what, let alone who, his parents were. But the little face peering from inside Fathomless Tilt's oversized diver's helmet isn't threatening; rather, he looks innocently curious. And his diving rig—made from aged and distressed suede and leather with two huge earpieces made from keys—confirms your first impression: Whatever his species, he's a full-fledged member of the steampunk tribe.

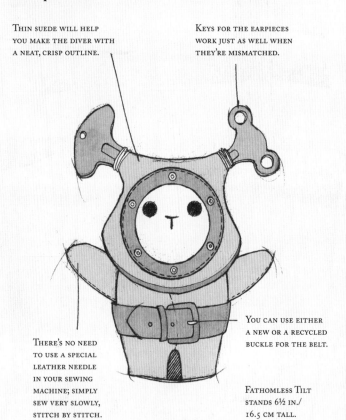

THIN SUEDE WILL HELP YOU MAKE THE DIVER WITH A NEAT, CRISP OUTLINE.

KEYS FOR THE EARPIECES WORK JUST AS WELL WHEN THEY'RE MISMATCHED.

THERE'S NO NEED TO USE A SPECIAL LEATHER NEEDLE IN YOUR SEWING MACHINE; SIMPLY SEW VERY SLOWLY, STITCH BY STITCH.

YOU CAN USE EITHER A NEW OR A RECYCLED BUCKLE FOR THE BELT.

FATHOMLESS TILT STANDS 6½ IN./ 16.5 CM TALL.

TO MAKE FATHOMLESS TILT

1 / Photocopy, or scan and print, the pattern pieces from pages 74-75 and cut them out.

2 / Following the instructions on page 6 and using candlewax, distress the suede and leather pieces. Distress a little more material than you will need so that you can use the pieces with the best aging for the most visible pieces of Fathomless.

3 / Lay the pattern pieces onto the suede (head front and back, body front and back, two body bases, and four arms) and leather (helmet ring and belt), and use the fabric pencil to draw around them. Cut the pieces out, leaving a ¼-in./6-mm allowance outside the pencil line, but do not cut out the face hole or helmet ring just yet.

TO MAKE THE BODY

4 / Coat the wrong sides of both base pieces with a thin layer of latex adhesive, leave to dry for a minute or two, then press together. Trim the seam allowance off around the pencil line to get a neat, double-thickness oval.

5 / Thread the sewing machine with yellow buttonhole thread and stitch the wavy line down the front of the body as marked (if you decide to sew the line by hand, use a medium-sized backstitch). Mark the leg division with a black felt-tip pen.

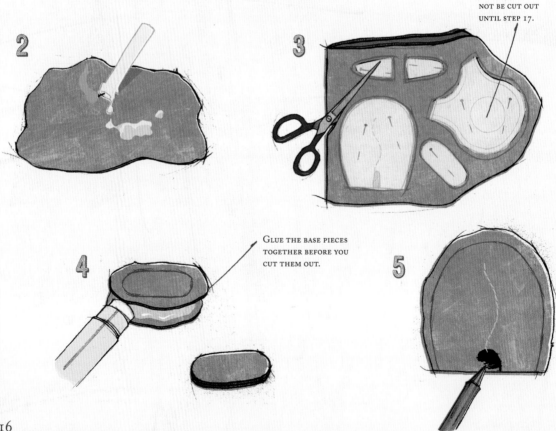

THIS HOLE WILL NOT BE CUT OUT UNTIL STEP 17.

GLUE THE BASE PIECES TOGETHER BEFORE YOU CUT THEM OUT.

6 / Thread the machine with gray thread, align two arm pieces together, and stitch around them, leaving the body end open for stuffing. Trim the seam allowance close to the stitching and pad the arm lightly with soft toy stuffing. Repeat to make the second arm.

7 / Lay the arms in position on the front body piece as shown.

8 / Put the front and back body pieces together, right sides facing. Sandwich the arms between the body pieces so that they will be on the right side when the body is turned out. Sew the back and front together, leaving the base open.

9 / Trim the body seam allowance, leaving the allowance uncut at the join of the arms and the body. Turn the body right side out.

10 / Fit the double-base piece into the open base of the body. Thread a needle with gray buttonhole thread and use a baseball stitch to hand sew the base into the body, leaving a small gap. Make a funnel from a small piece of paper and use it to pour toy-stuffing pellets into the body until it is firmly filled. Sew up the gap and fasten off the thread.

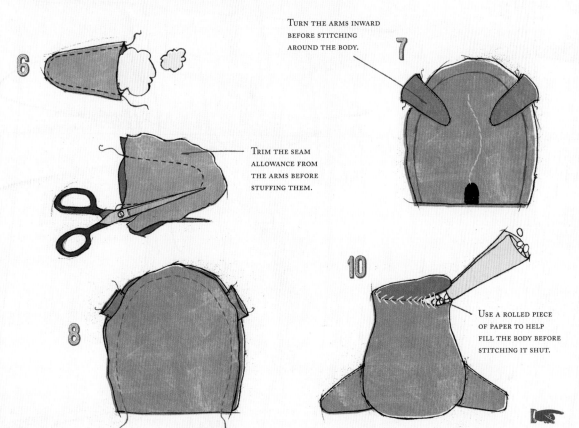

TURN THE ARMS INWARD BEFORE STITCHING AROUND THE BODY.

TRIM THE SEAM ALLOWANCE FROM THE ARMS BEFORE STUFFING THEM.

USE A ROLLED PIECE OF PAPER TO HELP FILL THE BODY BEFORE STITCHING IT SHUT.

11 / Fold the sides of the belt strip inward along the fold lines and use latex adhesive to glue them down.

12 / Use the hole punch to punch a hole in the center of the strip, push the pin of the buckle through it, then wrap the end around the buckle and fold down. Fold a tiny strip for the belt loop around the belt and glue down, then stick the folded belt-end down, securing both the buckle and the loop under it. Use the hole punch to make four holes where marked on the belt pattern.

13 / Wrap the belt around the body and secure. Thread the embroidery needle with three strands of beige buttonhole thread and stitch two cross-stitches on the back of the body to act as belt loops and hold it in place. Fasten off the thread inside the body.

TO MAKE THE HEAD

14 / Mark the holes for the helmet screws on the front face piece by laying the paper pattern over the face, drawing around it, and pushing through the marked points using the bradawl.

15 / Enlarge the holes to ⅛ in./3 mm diameter using a hole punch.

16 / Machine-stitch the darts in both head pieces using gray thread, then trim off the excess leather with scissors close to the stitching.

17 / Cut the hole marked on the pattern in the front head piece with scissors (there is no seam allowance).

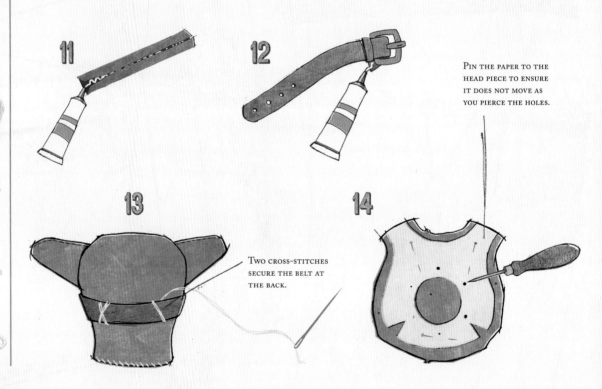

PIN THE PAPER TO THE HEAD PIECE TO ENSURE IT DOES NOT MOVE AS YOU PIERCE THE HOLES.

TWO CROSS-STITCHES SECURE THE BELT AT THE BACK.

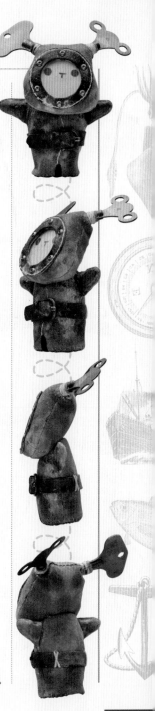

18 / With right sides together, sew the back and front of the head together, leaving the whole top edge of the head open. Trim the seam allowance close to the stitching, leaving the seam allowance on the top edge of the head on, to overlap and glue later. Turn the head right side out.

19 / To make the face, cut out one circle of cardstock, one of plastic (from the food container lid), and one of white cotton, using the outside of the helmet ring template for all three.

20 / Glue the cotton circle to the cardstock circle using a glue stick. Use the pink felt-tip pen to draw the eyes and the black felt-tip pen to draw the nose.

21 / Use a glue stick to run a thin line of glue around the edge of the clear plastic face circle, then stick it on top of the cardstock and cotton face pieces already glued together. When dry, mark for holes through the paper pattern using the bradawl, and then punch ⅛ in./3 mm holes with the hole punch through all three layers.

22 / Cut a flat piece of plastic from the side of the milk carton, then mark the helmet ring pattern on it and cut it out. Mark the helmet ring pattern onto the back of the leather leaving a ¼ in/6 mm seam allowance on the inside and outside edges. Spread a layer of contact adhesive over the back of the leather piece, and another on one side of the plastic. Leave a few minutes to dry, then stick the leather to the plastic. Make snips inside the ring on the leather.

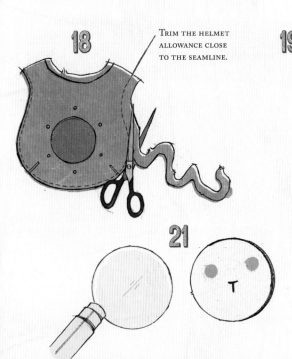

18

TRIM THE HELMET ALLOWANCE CLOSE TO THE SEAMLINE.

19

21

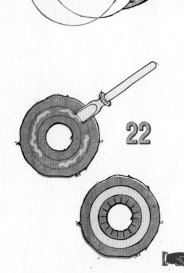

22

23 / Put some contact adhesive on the back of the plastic ring and leave to dry for 2 to 3 minutes, then wrap the leather around the inner edge and glue to the back. Trim the leather on the outer edge flush with the plastic.

24 / Thread the sewing machine with yellow buttonhole thread on the top and gray thread on the bobbin and stitch around the ring's outside edge. You will find it easier to turn the machine slowly by hand and make a stitch or two at a time.

25 / Mark holes through the pattern onto the helmet ring with the bradawl, then enlarge them to ⅛ in./3 mm diameter with the hole punch.

26 / Push the screws through the holes in the helmet ring, then through the corresponding holes in the head front. Place the face circle inside the head and push it onto the screw shanks from inside. Use your fingers and pliers to attach the nuts onto the screws inside the head, holding the nuts still with the pliers. Tighten the screw heads on the front of the helmet ring by turning the Allen wrench in circles.

27 / Fill the head with soft toy stuffing through the open gap at the top. Spread a thin layer of contact adhesive on both of the "ear" key shafts and on the leather keyholes, allow to dry for a few minutes, and stick the keys in place.

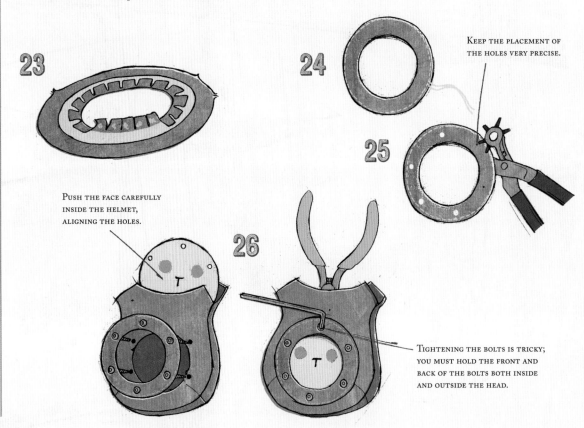

KEEP THE PLACEMENT OF THE HOLES VERY PRECISE.

PUSH THE FACE CAREFULLY INSIDE THE HELMET, ALIGNING THE HOLES.

TIGHTENING THE BOLTS IS TRICKY; YOU MUST HOLD THE FRONT AND BACK OF THE BOLTS BOTH INSIDE AND OUTSIDE THE HEAD.

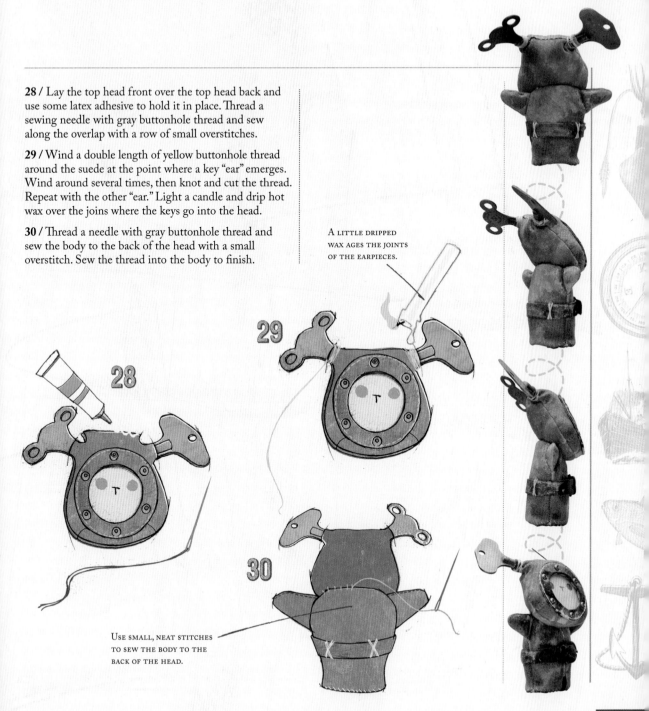

28 / Lay the top head front over the top head back and use some latex adhesive to hold it in place. Thread a sewing needle with gray buttonhole thread and sew along the overlap with a row of small overstitches.

29 / Wind a double length of yellow buttonhole thread around the suede at the point where a key "ear" emerges. Wind around several times, then knot and cut the thread. Repeat with the other "ear." Light a candle and drip hot wax over the joins where the keys go into the head.

30 / Thread a needle with gray buttonhole thread and sew the body to the back of the head with a small overstitch. Sew the thread into the body to finish.

A LITTLE DRIPPED WAX AGES THE JOINTS OF THE EARPIECES.

USE SMALL, NEAT STITCHES TO SEW THE BODY TO THE BACK OF THE HEAD.

MARVELETTA O'HOULIHAN

MATERIALS & EQUIPMENT
- Pinstriped gray wool fabric, 10 x 4 in./25 x 10 cm
- Gray felt, 2 x 2 in./5 x 5 cm
- Cream cotton calico, 2¾ x 8¼ in./7 x 21 cm
- Pale blue stretch wool fabric, 8 x 4 in./20 x 10 cm
- White felt, 3 x 2 in./7.5 x 5 cm
- Sewing thread in white, gray, and pale blue
- Medium-size bead cap
- Small diamanté stone, about 6 mm diameter
- Small metal tea ball with handle
- Funnel-shaped metal blind pull weights (or funnel-shaped metal beads) about ¾ in./2 cm long
- Clear glass bead, 10 mm diameter
- Flower-shaped metal bead (or bead cap), 10 mm diameter
- Fine brass or brass-colored chain, 4 in./10 cm length
- Brass or brass-colored trigger clasp, ½ in./12 mm long
- 3 round, ridged silver beads, 3 mm diameter
- 1 brass bugle bead, 10 mm long
- 1 eye pin, 1½ in./4 cm long
- 1 elaborate lantern-shaped bead, 1 in./2.5 cm long
- 1 brass disc-shaped bead, 10 mm diameter
- 2 jump rings, 6 mm diameter
- 1 tiny blue glass bead
- 1 round-ended safety pin, ⅞ in./2 cm long
- Packet of small plastic toy-filling pellets
- Small quantity of soft toy stuffing
- Piece of cardstock (postcard weight), 2 x 2 in./5 x 5 cm
- Latex adhesive
- Epoxy glue
- Superglue
- PVA glue
- Fabric pencil
- Fine felt-tip pens in red and black
- Sharp scissors
- Sewing needle
- Dressmaking pins
- Small hacksaw
- Bradawl
- Fine-nosed pliers

Note: You can make Marveletta entirely by hand sewing, but some parts are easier to sew on a machine.

Marveletta, the Steampunk Lady, has plenty of natural breeding: her neat little collar, smartly tailored clothing, and exquisitely detailed opera glasses tell you that this is not a girl to be trifled with. She's not as tough to make as you might imagine—despite her polish and a plethora of well-bred accessories, she rests on a surprisingly solid and simple base, and her apparent complexity comes with the addition of a few cute details.

THE HAIR IS MADE OF STRETCH WOOLEN FABRIC, SO EASE THE SEAMS WHEN YOU TURN IT RIGHT SIDE OUT TO MAINTAIN THE SHAPE.

DRAW THE FEATURES ON CAREFULLY, ONE TINY STROKE AT A TIME, TO KEEP THEM DELICATE.

THE OPERA GLASSES ARE COMPOSED AS A UNIT BEFORE THEY ARE ADDED TO THE FIGURE.

MARVELETTA O'HOULIHAN STANDS 5 IN./ 13 CM TALL.

TO MAKE MARVELETTA O'HOULIHAN

1 / Photocopy, or scan and print, the pattern pieces from page 74 and cut them out.

TO MAKE THE BODY

2 / If you've only been able to find a pinstripe that is too wide for the scale of the figure (a very fine pinstripe can be hard to find), you can machine sew additional stripes between the existing ones in a matching thread to make a finer stripe that will work better with her scale. Measure the stripes before you sew to make sure that your pinstripes are even.

3 / Draw four body panels on the pinstriped fabric. Make sure that the stripes are going straight up and down on each piece. One piece has an additional stitched "cape edge" detail, so on one of the pattern pieces, line a fabric stripe up with the cape edge stripe shown on the pattern. Cut out, allowing a ⅜ in./1 cm seam allowance around each piece.

4 / Thread the sewing machine with white thread and stitch three extra parallel lines directly next to each other on the body piece with the marked cape edge. This will give the effect of an additional fabric edge on that body piece.

5 / Thread the sewing machine with gray sewing thread and sew the panels together along their long edges to form a cone shape. Trim the seam allowance on the sewn edges to ⅛ in./3 mm.

6 / Draw around the body base pattern on the pinstriped material and cut the base out, allowing a ⅜ in./1 cm seam allowance around it. Pin the base into the large open end of the body cone, right sides in. Match the edges of the panels to the quarter points marked on the pattern.

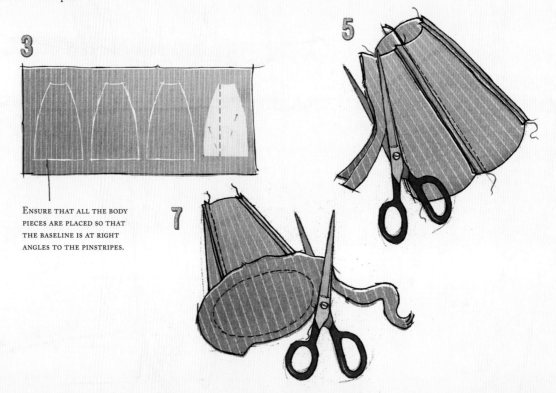

ENSURE THAT ALL THE BODY PIECES ARE PLACED SO THAT THE BASELINE IS AT RIGHT ANGLES TO THE PINSTRIPES.

7 / Sew the base into the body with gray thread either by machine or by hand a small backstitch. Trim the seam allowance to ⅛ in./3 mm.

8 / Turn the body right side out. Fill it with toy-filling pellets until it is tightly packed. Turn the seam allowance on the neck into the body, and finish stuffing the body with a few wisps of soft toy stuffing.

9 / Cut the gray felt into two pieces and glue them together with latex adhesive—spread a thin layer on each piece, leave to dry for a couple of minutes, then press together. Draw around the pattern piece for the body plug and cut it out of the felt—it does not need a seam allowance.

10 / Push the felt piece into the top of the body and hand sew it in place using gray thread and a small overstitch.

TO MAKE THE HEAD

11 / Cut the strip of cream calico into three squares, each 2¾ x 2¾ in./7 x 7 cm.

12 / Stack the three squares together and arrange the pattern piece for the face on it so that the weave of the fabric is crosswise on the pattern (that is, so that the face circle is on the bias of the fabric). Draw around the pattern piece.

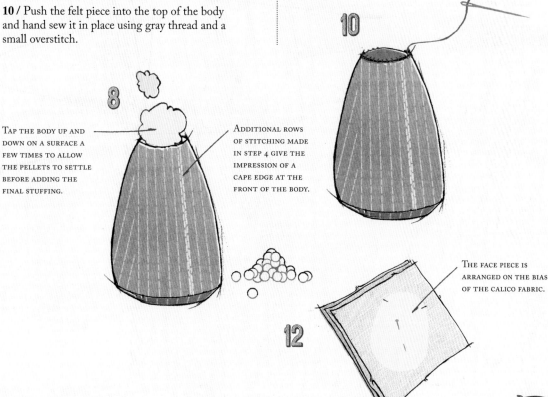

TAP THE BODY UP AND DOWN ON A SURFACE A FEW TIMES TO ALLOW THE PELLETS TO SETTLE BEFORE ADDING THE FINAL STUFFING.

ADDITIONAL ROWS OF STITCHING MADE IN STEP 4 GIVE THE IMPRESSION OF A CAPE EDGE AT THE FRONT OF THE BODY.

THE FACE PIECE IS ARRANGED ON THE BIAS OF THE CALICO FABRIC.

13 / Using matching thread, sew along the pattern line through all three layers of calico, leaving the top of the face open between the marks on the pattern. Knot off the thread and trim around the seam, leaving a ⅜ in./ 1 cm seam allowance.

14 / Use the labeled pattern piece to cut the cardstock for inside the face. Do not leave a seam allowance.

15 / Gently push the cardstock face between the second and third layers of calico. Lightly pad the shape by pushing small wisps of soft toy stuffing between the first and second layers of calico. When the padding is evenly arranged, sew the gap shut.

16 / Use the pattern of the face shape to lightly outline the face area on the fabric with a fabric pencil.

17 / Cut the pale blue wool fabric into two squares, each 4 x 4 in./10 x 10 cm. Align them, right sides together, and draw around the hair pattern on the top square with a fabric pencil (cut the face shape out on the template and outline this with pencil, too). Sew the fabric together along the pattern line, leaving the neck open. Trim around the stitching, leaving a ⅛ in./3 mm seam allowance, and snip the allowance toward the stitching at the sharp angles of the hair shape with scissors, taking care not to snip the stitching.

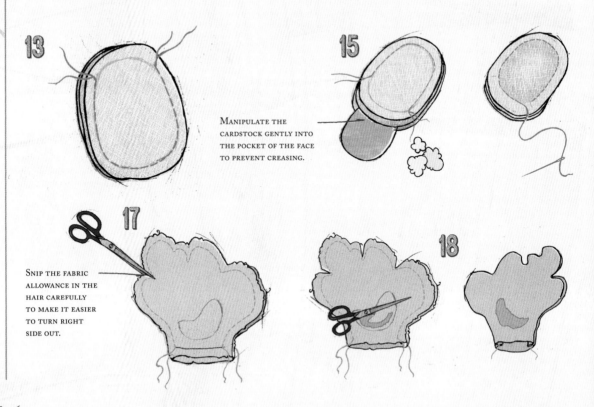

MANIPULATE THE CARDSTOCK GENTLY INTO THE POCKET OF THE FACE TO PREVENT CREASING.

SNIP THE FABRIC ALLOWANCE IN THE HAIR CAREFULLY TO MAKE IT EASIER TO TURN RIGHT SIDE OUT.

18 / Cut the face shape out of the front of the hair and turn the hair right side out.

19 / Push the face into the hair pocket. Thread a sewing needle with pale blue thread, align the face on the calico with the face window cut from the hair, and stitch the hair around the face, turning in the seam allowance as you go and using small, neat catching stitches. Finish off the thread inside the hair.

20 / Stuff the head with soft toy stuffing until it is well padded. Try to get some stuffing along the face/hairline in the forehead area. Turn in the seam allowance on the neck, thread a needle with pale blue thread and sew a line of running stitches around the open edge of the neck. Align it with the top of the body, gather up the thread, and when the base of the neck is the same diameter as the top of the body, knot the thread.

21 / Use pliers or your fingers to open up the bead cap to make the hair ornament. Stick the diamanté stone in the center of the cap with superglue and use pale green thread to stitch the ornament in place on the hair.

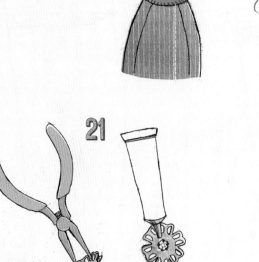

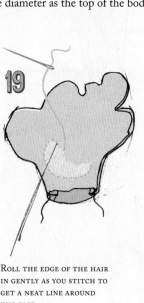

ROLL THE EDGE OF THE HAIR IN GENTLY AS YOU STITCH TO GET A NEAT LINE AROUND THE FACE.

22 / Mark the mouth and eye with the fine red and black felt-tip pens.

23 / Thread a needle with pale green thread and stitch the head to the body using a small overstitch.

24 / Using the collar pattern, cut the collar from the white felt and use PVA glue to stick it in place around the top of the body, overlapping and gluing it at the back of the neck.

TO MAKE THE OPERA GLASSES AND THE LANTERN-SHAPED EVENING BAG

25 / Use the hacksaw to cut the segment shown from the tea ball handle. The section should be about 2¾ in./7 cm long. Use superglue to fix the flexible joint at a right angle and leave to dry.

26 / Glue the small ends of the two funnel-shaped blind pulls onto the arm of the opera glasses with epoxy glue, and allow to dry. Add a drop of glue at the point at which the "glasses" touch at their wider ends and leave to dry. Add superglue to one side of the clear glass bead and to one side of the flower bead, and drop each bead into one "eye" of the opera glasses.

27 / When the opera glasses are completely dry, fix one end of the chain to the ring of the trigger clasp and clip the clasp to the top of the opera glasses' handle. Thread and stick one of the ridged silver beads onto the handle just under the clasp, leave ¾ in./2 cm of the handle clear, then glue on a second silver bead, the straight bugle bead, and the final silver bead.

CUT THE "ARM" AND JOINT OF THE OPERA GLASSES FROM ONE SIDE OF THE TEA BALL'S HANDLE.

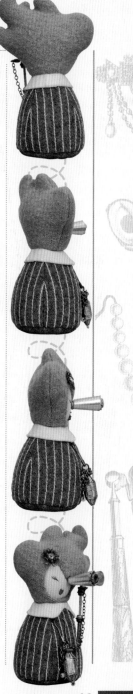

27

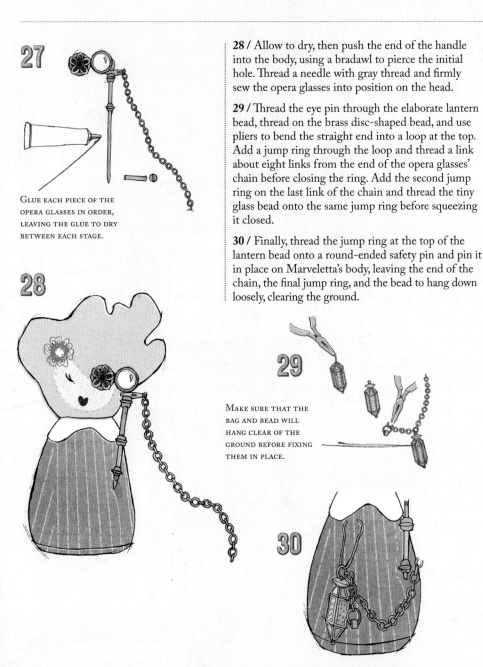

GLUE EACH PIECE OF THE
OPERA GLASSES IN ORDER,
LEAVING THE GLUE TO DRY
BETWEEN EACH STAGE.

28 / Allow to dry, then push the end of the handle into the body, using a bradawl to pierce the initial hole. Thread a needle with gray thread and firmly sew the opera glasses into position on the head.

29 / Thread the eye pin through the elaborate lantern bead, thread on the brass disc-shaped bead, and use pliers to bend the straight end into a loop at the top. Add a jump ring through the loop and thread a link about eight links from the end of the opera glasses' chain before closing the ring. Add the second jump ring on the last link of the chain and thread the tiny glass bead onto the same jump ring before squeezing it closed.

30 / Finally, thread the jump ring at the top of the lantern bead onto a round-ended safety pin and pin it in place on Marveletta's body, leaving the end of the chain, the final jump ring, and the bead to hang down loosely, clearing the ground.

28

29

MAKE SURE THAT THE
BAG AND BEAD WILL
HANG CLEAR OF THE
GROUND BEFORE FIXING
THEM IN PLACE.

30

GERONIMO BORE

MATERIALS & EQUIPMENT

- Dark denim, approximately 14 x 6 in./35 x 15 cm
- Beige suede, 10 x 5 in./25 x 13 cm
- Thin brown leather, 7 x 4 in./18 x 10 cm
- Scrap of metallic leatherette (or plastic fabric), 6 x 3 in./15 x 7.5 cm
- Handkerchief (or small scarf), ideally with a corner pattern or border
- Maroon grosgrain ribbon, $\frac{1}{8}$ in./3 mm diameter, 6 in./15 cm long
- Sewing thread in navy, beige, green, and black
- Buttonhole thread in orange and beige
- Bright green embroidery floss
- 32 black craft brads, $\frac{1}{8}$ in./3 mm diameter
- Large plastic snap fastener, $\frac{5}{8}$ in./15 mm diameter
- Green button, $\frac{3}{4}$ in./2 cm diameter
- Brass curtain ring, 1 in./2.5 cm diameter
- Round black bead, $\frac{1}{4}$ in./6 mm diameter
- Hexagonal screw bolt, 3 in./6.5 cm long
- 2 brass eyelets, $\frac{3}{16}$ in./4 mm diameter
- "Tools" for the toolbelt—see note at Step 33
- Small scrap of heavy cardstock, 3 x 2 in./7.5 x 5 cm
- Packet of small plastic toy-filling pellets
- Small quantity of soft toy stuffing
- Plastic milk carton
- Small plastic bottle (such as a travel cosmetics bottle), approximately 3 in./8.5 cm high
- Black cord elastic, $\frac{1}{8}$ in./3 mm diameter, 4 in./10 cm length
- Contact adhesive
- Latex adhesive
- Superglue
- PVA glue
- Acrylic paint in black and gold
- Light colored fabric pencil
- Permanent marker pen in green
- Dark brown chalk crayon
- Black ballpoint pen
- Sharp scissors
- Sewing and embroidery needles
- Dressmaking pins
- Bradawl
- Craft knife or hacksaw
- Small piece of fine sandpaper
- Small paintbrush
- Small craft drill (optional)

If you're a prospector by trade, it helps to have some built-in strengths. Geronimo's is his drill arm—never has a man been so firmly attached to his tools. His style suits his profession, too: heavy denim dungarees, a jaunty bandana and some hefty shoulder armor all add to his rugged appeal. Rumor has it that although he made his fortune long, long ago, he can't give up his quest for the glittery things you find in rocks. Nuggets of gold, copper, phrenite, and iron dance before him in his dreams.

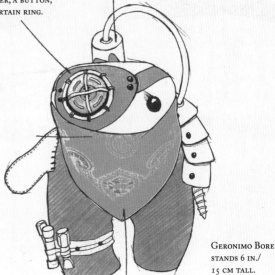

DESPITE THE EYE PATCH'S COMPLEX APPEARANCE, IT'S SIMPLY MADE FROM A SCRAP OF LEATHER, A BUTTON, AND A CURTAIN RING.

BLACK AND GOLD ACRYLIC PAINT ARE MIXED WITH PVA GLUE TO "AGE" GERONIMO'S TANK.

GERONIMO BORE STANDS 6 IN./ 15 CM TALL.

USE THE EDGE OF A STANDARD-SIZED BANDANA TO GET A CORNER PATTERN FOR THE SCARF.

Note: Some parts of Geronimo are much easier to sew on a sewing machine.

TO MAKE GERONIMO BORE

1 / Photocopy, or scan and print, the pattern pieces from page 75 and cut them out.

TO MAKE THE BODY

2 / Turn the dark denim wrong side up and use a fabric pencil to draw around the body pattern piece on it twice. Turn the pattern piece wrong side up and draw around it two more times (you're making a tiny pair of dungarees!). Cut all four pieces out, leaving a ¼ in./ 6 mm seam allowance.

3 / Arrange the body pieces in two pairs, right sides together, and sew the outside seam of each with navy thread, starting at the top mark shown on the pattern and extending into the seam allowance at the end of the trouser leg.

4 / To topstitch the leg seams, open the stitched pieces out flat and fold the seam allowance under on the seam you're going to stitch on the first leg. Mark the end of the stitching detail shown on the pattern with a pin. Thread the sewing machine with orange buttonhole thread on top and navy sewing thread in the bobbin, set a long stitch, and sew a line from the marking pin to the end of the leg, stitching back and forth to strengthen the seam at both ends. Repeat for the other leg.

Note: Fold the seam allowance and sew the stitching detail down the right-hand side of the seam on one leg and on the left-hand side on the other.

5 / Fold the legs right sides together and pin and stitch the inside seams with navy thread, extending into both seam allowances. Pin the legs together, right sides in, and stitch fronts to backs.

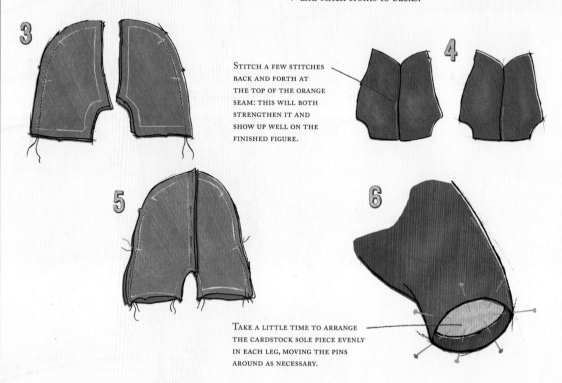

STITCH A FEW STITCHES BACK AND FORTH AT THE TOP OF THE ORANGE SEAM: THIS WILL BOTH STRENGTHEN IT AND SHOW UP WELL ON THE FINISHED FIGURE.

TAKE A LITTLE TIME TO ARRANGE THE CARDSTOCK SOLE PIECE EVENLY IN EACH LEG, MOVING THE PINS AROUND AS NECESSARY.

6 / Turn the dungarees right side out. Draw around the foot pattern twice on the cardstock and cut the foot pieces out. Push a cardstock piece up ⅜ in./1 cm into each leg and pin from the outside, through the denim and into the edge of the cardstock, to hold it in place.

7 / Spread a thin layer of contact adhesive on the cardstock at the end of each leg and another on the denim at the lower inside of each leg, up as far as the cardstock. Leave to dry for a few minutes, then stick the denim down over the cardstock on each leg, working from the outside edge of the foot inwards and pushing the excess denim into small, neat tucks.

8 / Pour plastic toy-filling pellets into the legs and body to about 1 in./2.5 cm of the top. Fill the top part with soft toy stuffing. When the body is quite tightly packed, turn in the seam allowance at the top and hand sew the top of the body closed using navy thread and a small overstitch.

TO MAKE THE HEAD AND ARMS

9 / Draw around the head pattern twice on the wrong side of the beige suede. Mark the center hole shown on the pattern on one piece only (this is the back of the head). Cut out the head pieces and the center hole, leaving a ¼ in./6 mm seam allowance. Don't cut down into the notches for the darts.

10 / Sew along the darts with beige thread, then cut the excess off close to the stitching line. Place the right sides together and sew around the outside of the head. Trim the seam allowance, turn the right side out through the hole in the back, and fill with soft toy stuffing.

11 / Cut two small pieces of suede, each a little larger than the arm pattern piece. Put one on top of the other, right sides out, and draw around the pattern with a fabric pencil. Sew around the line with beige thread and trim close to the stitching. Fill with soft toy stuffing.

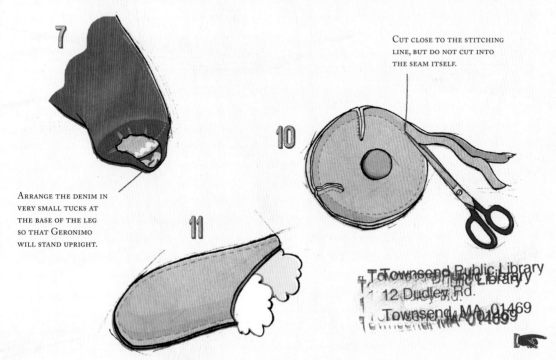

CUT CLOSE TO THE STITCHING LINE, BUT DO NOT CUT INTO THE SEAM ITSELF.

ARRANGE THE DENIM IN VERY SMALL TUCKS AT THE BASE OF THE LEG SO THAT GERONIMO WILL STAND UPRIGHT.

12 / Draw the eye patch pattern and its strap onto the brown leather and cut the two pieces out. Spread the back of the patch and the front of the patch part of the strap with a thin layer of latex adhesive. Leave to dry for a few minutes, then stick the patch onto the strap. Use the bradawl to make two small holes on each side of the patch and insert ⅛ in./3 mm brads into the holes. Open the backs of the brads to hold them in place.

13 / Open the plastic snap fastener and color the half that has a central hole with the green permanent marker pen. Use a tiny drop of super glue to stick the half-snap on top of the button. When set, hand sew the button/snap component onto the eye patch with green thread.

14 / Thread a needle with a double strand of orange buttonhole thread and stitch the curtain ring onto the patch around the button with eight stitches, spaced at even intervals.

15 / Thread a needle with a full thickness of bright green embroidery floss and stitch a cross over the center of the button, passing the thread between the edge of the button and the inside of the curtain ring.

16 / Use the dark brown chalk crayon to draw a smudged line on the left side of the head to make the left eye "socket." Thread a needle with black thread and sew the black bead in place, taking the thread through to the back of the head and pulling it tight to create a hollow around the "eye."

17 / Place the eye patch and strap on the head and mark its place lightly with the fabric pencil, then spread the back of the patch and strap and its spot on the head with a thin layer of latex adhesive. Leave to dry for a few minutes, then press the patch into place around the head.

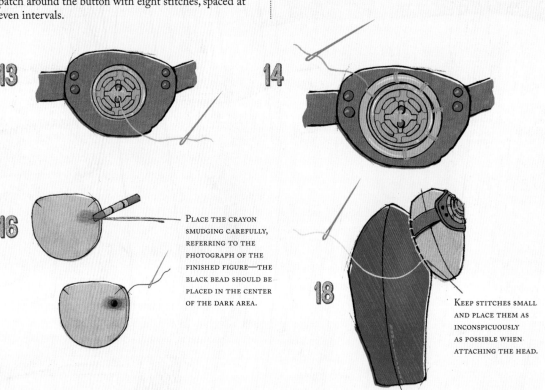

PLACE THE CRAYON SMUDGING CAREFULLY, REFERRING TO THE PHOTOGRAPH OF THE FINISHED FIGURE—THE BLACK BEAD SHOULD BE PLACED IN THE CENTER OF THE DARK AREA.

KEEP STITCHES SMALL AND PLACE THEM AS INCONSPICUOUSLY AS POSSIBLE WHEN ATTACHING THE HEAD.

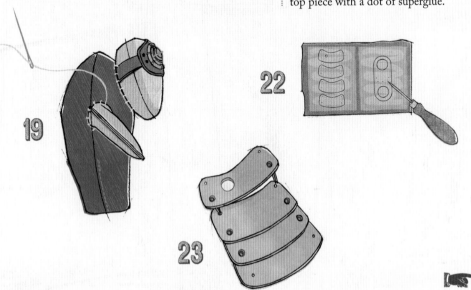

18 / Sew the head onto the body using beige thread and a small overstitch. The head should stand ½ in./12 mm higher than the top of the body and the line of stitching should be about ⅝ in./15 mm down from the seam on the back of the head.

19 / Thread a needle with beige buttonhole thread and sew on the right arm. It should be attached about 2¾ in./7 cm from the floor when the figure is standing.

20 / Sew the bolt in position to make the left arm, using beige buttonhole thread and stitching just below the head of the screw.

TO MAKE THE ARMOR AND THE TANK

21 / Cut some flat pieces from the sides of the plastic milk carton, enough to accommodate four armor pieces and one tank mount. Cut corresponding pieces from the metallic leatherette. Lightly sand the plastic to roughen it, then spread a layer of contact adhesive on the back of the metallic fabric and the front of the plastic pieces. Leave to dry for a few minutes, then stick the metallic fabric onto the plastic.

22 / Use a black ballpoint pen to draw around the armor pattern four times and the tank mount pattern once on the sandwiched fabric/plastic. Mark the dots on the pattern pieces and use a bradawl to mark them on the fabric. Only one of the armor pieces needs the larger (³/₁₆ in./4 mm) hole cut into it. Cut all the pieces out.

23 / Use the bradawl to enlarge the holes on all the cut pieces. Use a craft knife to level the plastic on the back of the pieces where the bradawl was pushed through. Keeping the armor piece with the ³/₁₆ in./4 mm hole topmost, fix the other pieces underlapping it, each attached with two brads pushed through the piece above and opened at the back. Create the curve in the armor by pinching it in half horizontally. Glue the ⅛ in./3 mm brass eyelet into the larger hole on the top piece with a dot of superglue.

24 / Push three brads through the marked holes in the tank mount and open them at the back. Stitch the mount to the body through the marked stitching holes using navy sewing thread and lining it up along the seam in the middle of the body back.

25 / Rub the plastic bottle to be used for the tank all over with fine sandpaper and use a bradawl to pierce a hole in the top of the lid. Enlarge it until it is ³/₁₆ in./4 mm in diameter. (You can do this carefully with a bradawl and a sharp scissor blade or use a small drill.) Glue the second brass eyelet in the hole with a dot of superglue.

26 / Mark a row of dots around the bottom edge of the lid, pierce them with a bradawl, then put a ¹/₈ in./3 mm brad in each hole. Use superglue to fix one end of the black cord elastic inside the lid, feeding it through the eyelet hole.

27 / Mix a very little black with gold acrylic paint for a vintage look, and add a few drops of PVA glue. Mix well, then paint the elastic, lid, and bottle and leave to dry.

28 / Thread a needle with navy thread, then position the armor piece over the screw, pinning it onto the body through the empty holes in each corner. Stitch the armor to the body through these holes and finish by pushing a brad into the lower holes, over the stitching, and opening them at the back.

29 / Push the bottle neck up through the two holes in the mount, then screw on the lid and carefully twist the bottle until the cord elastic is in a neat loop over the left shoulder. Feed the loose end of the elastic into the eyelet in the armor and super-glue it in place, trimming a little off the length as necessary.

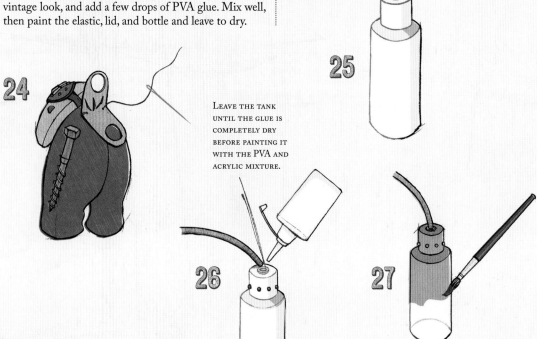

LEAVE THE TANK UNTIL THE GLUE IS COMPLETELY DRY BEFORE PAINTING IT WITH THE PVA AND ACRYLIC MIXTURE.

TO MAKE THE FINISHING TOUCHES

30 / To make the scarf, trace around the pattern piece twice. Make sure that one piece takes in the patterned corner of the scarf (this will be the pointed end that you see around the face). Cut the two pieces out, align them, right sides together, and use matching thread to sew around the edge, leaving a small hole to turn right side out. Turn the scarf right side out, press, and hand sew the small opening closed.

31 / Pin the scarf onto the front of the figure, wrong side out and upside down, and use matching thread to overstitch the scarf's edge to the front of the face. Fasten off the thread, pull the scarf down, then tie the loose ends at the back of the head with a small knot. Secure at the sides and back of the head with small, invisible stitches.

32 / For the toolbelt, cut a strip of thin brown leather ¾ in./2 cm wide and spread a layer of contact adhesive over the wrong side. Leave to dry for a few minutes, then fold the long edges to the center of the strip and press down. Turn the belt over and lay the strip of maroon grosgrain ribbon down the center. (It should extend further than each end.) Starting 1⅜ in./3.5 cm from one end, press the bradawl through both ribbon and leather, push a brad through the hole, and open it at the back.

33 / Your "tools" could be mini drill bits, fuses, or tiny nuts and bolts—use whatever you can find at a craft or hardware store. After you have fixed the first brad, lay the first tool on the belt, lay the ribbon over it, and use the bradawl to make a hole so that it can be fixed in place with a second brad. Repeat with the other tools, fixing them in place with more brads, and finish with a final brad at each end of the leather strip to hold the ribbon in place. Tie the toolbelt around the right leg with the ribbon and fix it in place with a few tiny stitches.

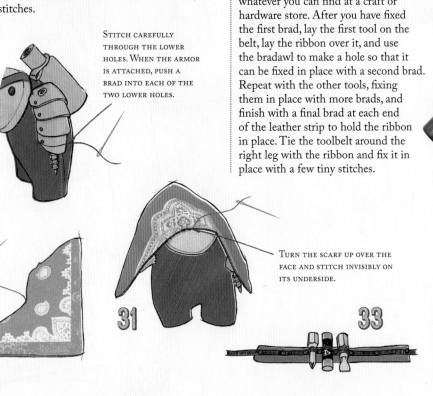

STITCH CAREFULLY THROUGH THE LOWER HOLES. WHEN THE ARMOR IS ATTACHED, PUSH A BRAD INTO EACH OF THE TWO LOWER HOLES.

TURN THE SCARF UP OVER THE FACE AND STITCH INVISIBLY ON ITS UNDERSIDE.

FLOYD FASTKNIGHT

MATERIALS & EQUIPMENT

- Piece of brown sheepskin with a ⅜ in./1 cm pile, 12 x 12 in./30 x 30 cm
- Black felt, 2 x 2¾ in./5 x 12 cm
- Beige cotton velvet (or short pile fabric), 4 x 4 in./10 x 10 cm
- Thin calico, 4 x 4 in./10 x 10 cm
- Rust leather, 5½ x 5½ in./14 x 14 cm
- Dark gray felt, 4¾ x 4 in./12 x 10 cm
- Thick beige leather, suede on one side, 4½ x 7¼ in./11 x 18 cm
- Buttonhole thread in brown and beige
- Sewing thread in beige, gray, and green
- Embroidery floss in dark gray
- Large black sequin, ¾ in./2 cm diameter
- Beer bottle cap
- Pack of mixed-color ⅛ in./3 mm craft brads
- Thin brass curtain ring, 1 in./2.5 cm diameter
- Toy compass, 1 in./2.5 cm diameter
- Strip of curtain weights, 8 in./20 cm length
- Small antiqued toggle fastener (jewelry finding) 1 in./2.5 cm long
- 2 curved gold metal beads, 1 in./2.5 cm long
- Small gold lobster clasp (jewelry finding)
- 3 jump rings, 2 x ¼ in./6 mm diameter, 1 x ½ in./12 mm diameter
- 2 small keys, approximately 1⅜ in./3.5 cm long
- Metal calligraphy pen with wooden handle
- Thin beige string, 30 in./75 cm long
- 2 fish-shaped metal beads, 1 in./2.5 cm long
- Small safety pin, ideally keyhole-shaped
- Piece of thin cardstock, 4¾ x 4 in./12 x 10 cm
- Plastic milk carton
- Small quantity of soft toy stuffing
- Scraps of paper to make rolled-up charts. (We used gridded paper, thick-texture cream paper and a scrap of a black-and-white photocopy.) You need about 3½ x 3½ in./ 9 x 9 cm of each type.
- Contact adhesive
- Glue stick
- Superglue
- Epoxy glue
- Light and dark fabric pencils
- Black permanent marker pen

Weighed down by maps and charts and warmly dressed against the Arctic cold (or insulated against the searing heat of the desert—take your pick; he's visited them all), Floyd Fastknight is renowned as an explorer in every geographical society on earth. Of course, he's got some natural advantages: his eyes are a clock and compass, and his soft, flat feet, like a camel's, can traverse any and every terrain. He's also got undoubted presence, Floyd. The ladies flock to his magic lantern lectures.

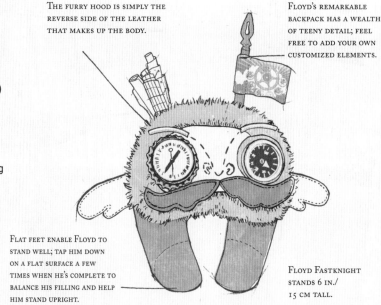

THE FURRY HOOD IS SIMPLY THE REVERSE SIDE OF THE LEATHER THAT MAKES UP THE BODY.

FLOYD'S REMARKABLE BACKPACK HAS A WEALTH OF TEENY DETAIL; FEEL FREE TO ADD YOUR OWN CUSTOMIZED ELEMENTS.

FLAT FEET ENABLE FLOYD TO STAND WELL; TAP HIM DOWN ON A FLAT SURFACE A FEW TIMES WHEN HE'S COMPLETE TO BALANCE HIS FILLING AND HELP HIM STAND UPRIGHT.

FLOYD FASTKNIGHT STANDS 6 IN./ 15 CM TALL.

- Sharp scissors
- Sewing and embroidery needles
- Dressmaking pins
- Bradawl
- Small metal file
- Hole punch
- Small hacksaw

- Craft knife and ruler (optional)
- Clear cellophane tape
- Small piece of fine sandpaper

Note: Floyd is made from a mixture of hand and machine sewing.

TO MAKE FLOYD FASTKNIGHT

1 / Either photocopy, or scan and print, the pattern pieces from page 76 and cut them out.

TO MAKE THE BODY, FACE, AND BAG

2 / On the leather side of the sheepskin, draw around the front of body pattern with a dark fabric pencil, then turn the pattern piece over and draw around it again. Repeat with the back of body and the foot patterns, so that you have two of each. Measure out a strip 1 in./2.5 cm wide by 9½ in./24 cm long with the direction of the fur pile across the width of the pattern. Cut all the pieces out carefully, cutting through the leather only, not through the pile of the fur.

3 / Thread a needle with brown buttonhole thread and use a baseball stitch to sew the feet to the front body pieces on the leather side. Then, also with baseball stitch,

sew the corresponding back pieces to each of the front pieces. Sew along the inside of the leg first, then the outside of the leg from the foot end to the point marked B on the pattern piece. Knot the thread off. (Except where otherwise stated, use baseball stitch to join the other sheepskin pieces together.)

4 / When the left and right sides are complete, trim any fur poking out of the open ends of the feet flush with the bottom edge of the leather.

5 / Spread a thin layer of contact adhesive over one side of the black felt and one side of the thin cardstock. Leave to dry for a few minutes, then press firmly together to stick. On the cardstock side, draw around the pattern piece for the sole with a permanent marker, marking the dots by pushing through the pattern into the card with a bradawl. Turn the pattern piece over and repeat for the second sole. Push the bradawl through the holes to widen them, then cut the soles out.

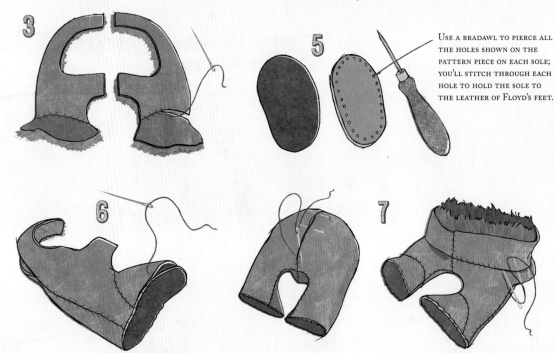

USE A BRADAWL TO PIERCE ALL THE HOLES SHOWN ON THE PATTERN PIECE ON EACH SOLE; YOU'LL STITCH THROUGH EACH HOLE TO HOLD THE SOLE TO THE LEATHER OF FLOYD'S FEET.

6 / With felt side out, pin the soles into the base of the feet, aligning the three side marks with the seams. Thread a needle with brown buttonhole thread and sew the soles to the feet, pushing the needle straight up through the holes in the felt and out through the sheepskin.

7 / Sew the two halves of the body together, including the two thin arched pieces on the body fronts. Stitch the long strip of sheepskin together at the ends to make a hoop shape and pin it onto the body with the seam at the bottom, and the fur pushing outward, away from the body. Sew it neatly in place.

8 / Roll the edge of the strip back and fold it in half; the exposed fur makes the trim of Floyd's hood. Use a needle threaded with brown buttonhole thread to catch the edge of the leather down along the seam between it and the body.

9 / Align the rectangles of velvet and calico, right sides together. Draw around the face pattern on the velvet, then sew around it on the sewing machine with beige thread, leaving the seam open between the two marks shown on the pattern piece. Cut the face out leaving a ⅛ in./3 mm seam allowance around the stitching and a slightly wider allowance around the open area. Turn the face right side out.

10 / Cut a piece of plastic from the side of the milk carton. Draw around the plastic face pattern piece with permanent marker and cut it out. Roll the plastic up and slide it into the opening in the face, then open it out flat. Pack the face between the plastic and the velvet with a little soft toy stuffing. When it is softly padded, use beige thread to neatly handstitch the gap shut.

11 / Photocopy, or scan and print, the clock face in the pattern pieces. This is to make Floyd's right eye. Use a glue stick to stick it onto some thin cardstock and cut it out, then cut a clock hand out of a large black sequin. Make a hole through the center of the beer bottle cap, the clock face, and the sequin hand with the bradawl. Assemble with a little superglue—stick the clock face and hand inside the bottle cap, and push a ⅛ in./3 mm black brad through the hole, opening it behind the bottle cap to hold it in place.

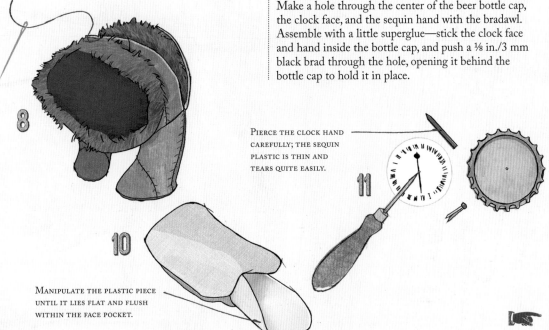

8

10

MANIPULATE THE PLASTIC PIECE UNTIL IT LIES FLAT AND FLUSH WITHIN THE FACE POCKET.

PIERCE THE CLOCK HAND CAREFULLY; THE SEQUIN PLASTIC IS THIN AND TEARS QUITE EASILY.

11

12 / With a bradawl, make three pairs of holes in the bottle cap, at the twelve, six, and three o'clock positions. Smooth down the protrusions on the outer edge of the cap with a metal file.

13 / Stick the curtain ring on top of the compass with a little super glue. Cut a strip from the rust leather that is the same depth as the compass and as long as its circumference. Spread a thin layer of contact adhesive around the edge of the compass and on the wrong side of the leather, wait a few minutes, and then press the leather in place around the compass.

14 / On the face, position the compass "eye" and clock "eye" off the edges of the face (check the photograph for placement), then sew them in place using brown buttonhole thread. Sew the right eye through the pairs of holes, starting from the back of the face and pushing the needle through the plastic and fabric layers, then through one of the pairs of holes and back through the face. Repeat twice, then stitch through the other two pairs of holes in the same way. For the left compass eye, start at the back of the face in the same way, but catch the edge of the leather eye surround. Make a stitch every ⅜ in./ 1 cm until you have sewn all the way round where the compass sits on the face.

15 / Fold the piece of dark gray felt in half, lay the two mustache pattern pieces on top of it, and draw around them with a light fabric pencil. Thread the machine with gray thread and stitch around both pieces leaving a small section open in each. Stuff the mustache pieces with a small amount of soft toy stuffing, then hand sew the opening shut. Cut the shapes out as close to the stitching as you can without cutting into it.

16 / Pin the mustache pieces on the face, marking their top point with a pin. Take them off, leaving the pin, and stitch the features with a needle threaded with three strands of dark gray embroidery floss, referring to the photograph for placement. Stitch the nose, just catching the stitches through the velvet. The sides of the nose are made with running stitches and the nostrils in backstitch with a French knot in the center of each nostril.

17 / Measure and cut two 4 in./10 cm lengths of curtain weights and push them down into Floyd's toes, then pack his legs with soft toy stuffing.

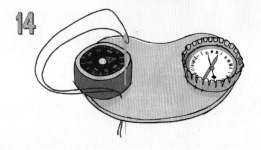

THREE PAIRS OF HOLES AT 12, 6, AND 3 O'CLOCK.

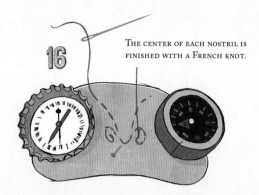

THE CENTER OF EACH NOSTRIL IS FINISHED WITH A FRENCH KNOT.

18 / Thread a needle with a doubled length of brown buttonhole thread, and stitch the edge of the face to the edge of the fur hood, placing a few stitches at each of the seven points, as shown below.

19 / Draw around the backpack pattern on the smooth side of the beige leather using a fabric pencil and cut it out. Use a hole punch to make two 1/8 in./3 mm holes at each end of the space for the slot, then use scissors to cut out the leather between the holes to make an oval opening.

20 / Thread a needle with a doubled length of beige buttonhole thread and use baseball stitch to sew one side of the backpack together, leaving the tabs outside of the pack; start at the right angle marked C on the pattern, and stitch the two edges together in a straight line until you get to the point marked D. Repeat on the other side. Next, fold the flap over the top of the backpack and mark a dot through the slot. Pad the backpack with soft toy stuffing, fold the flap back, and sew the toggle where the dot is marked.

21 / Use a bradawl to make two holes in each of the four tabs on the sides of the backpack. Place the backpack on the body back so that the top two tabs are about 3/8 in./ 1 cm from the sheepskin edge. Mark through the holes on the top tabs with a bradawl, pushing into the sheepskin. Widen the holes and attach the backpack on Floyd's back, pushing four brown craft brads into the holes. Repeat with the bottom tabs.

STITCH AT THE POINTS IN THE ORDER SHOWN TO ATTACH FLOYD'S FACE WITHIN HIS HOOD.

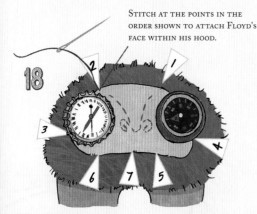

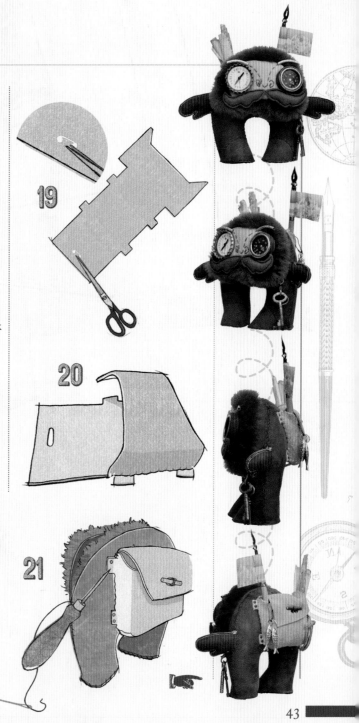

22 / Pack the rest of the body with soft toy stuffing and hand sew the open body closed using brown buttonhole thread.

TO FINISH THE EXPLORER

23 / Fold the remaining piece of rust leather in half. Draw around the glove pattern with a dark fabric pencil on the top surface, then turn the pattern piece over and draw around it again. Thread the sewing machine with beige buttonhole thread and sew around both outlines, leaving the wrist ends open. Cut both gloves out as close to the stitching as possible and fill with soft toy stuffing. Position the gloves along the side seams of the body, top edges ½ in./1 cm above the B mark and thumbs pointing down. Sew the gloves to the body with brown buttonhole thread.

24 / Sew the two mustache pieces on with gray sewing thread.

25 / Mix a small amount of the 2-part epoxy glue and glue a dressmaking pin inside one end of each of the curved metal tubular beads, sharp end outward. Leave to dry, then push the pins into the face at the top of the running-stitch nose lines to serve as eyebrows.

When they're in the right position, pull the pins almost back out, dot with superglue where they pierce the velvet, then push them back in and leave to dry.

26 / Add the lobster clasp to one of the small jump rings. Add the two keys to the clasp, then sew the jump ring in position on Floyd's left side, using brown buttonhole thread, so that the keys just clear the ground when he is standing.

27 / Use the hacksaw to cut the calligraphy pen to a length of 5 in./12.5 cm. Scan and print, or color-photocopy, the flag on the pattern page and cut it out with sharp scissors. Wrap the striped end around the pen, marking where the ends join, then remove it and sew a line with green thread on the sewing machine to make a tube at one end to push the pen through. Fix in place with a dot of superglue, bend a wave into the flag with your fingers, and push the pen into the left corner of the backpack.

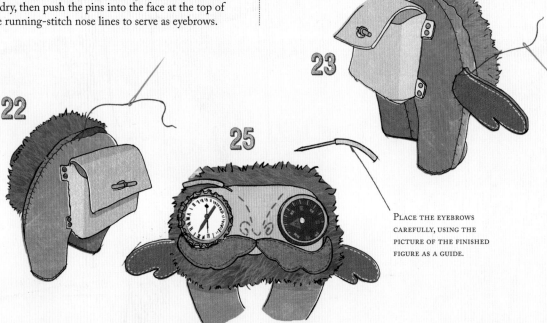

PLACE THE EYEBROWS CAREFULLY, USING THE PICTURE OF THE FINISHED FIGURE AS A GUIDE.

28 / Coil the string into a loop 1¾ in./4.5 cm in diameter and knot the ends together. Cut a tiny strip of beige leather, about ¾ x ¼ in./2 cm x 6 mm, and wrap it around the coil smooth side out. Use the bradawl to push holes through the end of the strip and the point marked E on the pattern, and push a gray brad through the hole in strip and into the hole in the backpack, opening it out inside the backpack.

29 / Thread a metal fish bead onto each of the remaining two jump rings and thread them onto the safety pin. Pin the safety pin through the bag, under the flap, near where the flag emerges.

30 / Roll up the three pieces of paper you've selected as charts, then crumple and "distress" them a little with your fingers. Join them together at the base with clear cellophane tape and push them into the right side of the backpack, folding the flap around them and using a dot of superglue to stick the flap in place.

BE SURE THE PEN WILL FIT THROUGH THE TUBE ON THE SIDE OF THE FLAG BEFORE STITCHING IT ON THE MACHINE.

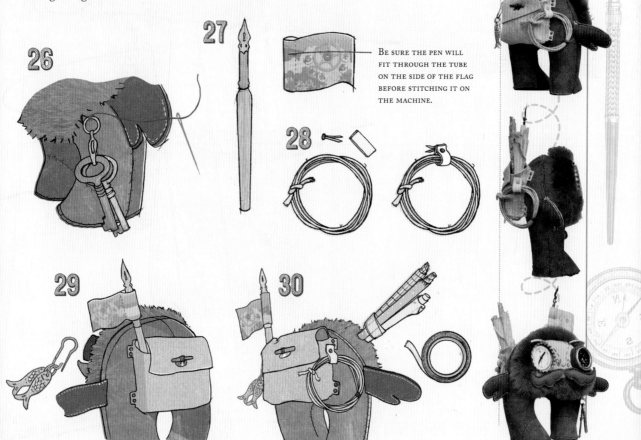

CHARITY STORM

MATERIALS & EQUIPMENT

- Purple wool fabric, 12 x 3 in./30 x 7.5 cm
- Metallic lace fabric (we used "antique gold")
  10 x 10 in./25 x 25 cm
- Thin brown leather, 2 x 3 in./5 x 7.5 cm
- Narrow-wale brown corduroy, 5 x 6 in./12.5 x 15 cm
- Small scrap of black felt
- Pink cotton poplin, 3 x 9 in./7.5 x 22.5 cm
- Pink knit fabric (or heavy jersey), 6 x 8 in./15 x 20 cm
- Sewing thread in purple, beige, black, brown, white,
  and pink
- Metallic sewing thread to match the color of the lace
- Buttonhole thread in beige
- Antique gold and bright green embroidery floss
- 4 tiny black metallic glass beads
- 2 pipe cleaners
- Silver jump ring, 1/4 in./6 mm diameter
- Small plastic ring, 5/8 in./1.5 cm diameter
- Packet of dark mixed color craft brads, 1/8 in./
  3 mm diameter
- 2 matching domed metal buttons,
  about 7/8 in./1.5 cm diameter
- 4 tiny tubular brass beads, about 1/8 in./3 mm diameter
- Piece of medium cardstock, 2 x 2 in./5 x 5 cm
- Piece of heavy (130 lb/300 gsm) patterned card.
  (For the wings, we chose wood-floor effect, but
  most craft stores will have a choice of patterns—
  something with parallel lines will work best.)
- Small piece of thick cream-colored paper
- Packet of small plastic toy-filling pellets
- Small quantity of soft toy stuffing
- Plain white candle
- Contact adhesive
- Superglue
- Light and dark fabric pencils
- Pencil
- Fine-tipped permanent marker in deep pink
- Sharp scissors
- Sewing needle
- Glass-headed dressmaking pins
- Compass
- Bradawl

Note: Charity is an even mix of hand
and machine sewing.

A dedicated aviatrix, Charity Storm has sprung her own pair of wings. She looks like a fantasy figure envisioned by the Wright brothers: hair whipped into a veritable banner by the wind, goggles firmly affixed, and speedometer set as high as it will go. A feminine flier, her neat little gauntlets boast pearl buttons, and she wears her lace overskirt with style. Few can keep up with her, though many have tried; her fan club has dubbed her the Spirit of Speed.

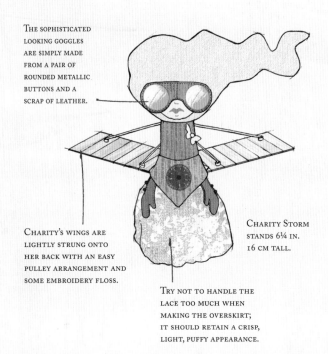

THE SOPHISTICATED LOOKING GOGGLES ARE SIMPLY MADE FROM A PAIR OF ROUNDED METALLIC BUTTONS AND A SCRAP OF LEATHER.

CHARITY'S WINGS ARE LIGHTLY STRUNG ONTO HER BACK WITH AN EASY PULLEY ARRANGEMENT AND SOME EMBROIDERY FLOSS.

CHARITY STORM STANDS 6¼ IN. 16 CM TALL.

TRY NOT TO HANDLE THE LACE TOO MUCH WHEN MAKING THE OVERSKIRT; IT SHOULD RETAIN A CRISP, LIGHT, PUFFY APPEARANCE.

TO MAKE CHARITY STORM

1 / Photocopy, or scan and print, the pattern pieces from page 77 and cut them out.

TO MAKE THE BODY AND ARMS

2 / Using a light fabric pencil, draw around the pattern for the body panel four times on the purple woolen fabric, drawing the side mark shown on the pattern on one of the four pieces. Draw around the pattern piece for the body base. Cut all the pieces out, leaving a ¼ in./ 6 mm seam allowance around each.

3 / Thread the sewing machine with purple thread and sew the four body panels together, right sides in, along the long edges. To complete the cone shape, on the fourth seam, stitch only as high as the mark on the pattern piece, leaving the neck end open. Trim the stitched seam allowance to ⅛ in./3 mm.

4 / Pin the base piece into the large open end of the body cone, matching the quarter points shown on the pattern piece to the seams of the body. Stitch the base in place, trim the seam allowance to ⅛ in./3 mm, and turn the body right side out. Fill with plastic toy-filling pellets as far as the seam opening.

5 / Thread a sewing needle with purple thread and fill the top part of the body with soft toy stuffing, packing tightly and sewing up the seam as you go. Sew through the top of the body, stitching the opening closed and leaving a small "stem" of neck about ¼ in./6 mm long at the top.

6 / Using the compass and a pencil, draw two concentric circles on a piece of paper, one 1⅝ in./4 cm in diameter and the other 9⅝ in./24 cm in diameter. Cut the ring out to make the pattern for the lace overskirt. Lay the pattern over the metallic lace and cut it out. (You do not need to leave a seam allowance.) Thread a sewing needle with beige thread and stitch a running stitch ¼ in./6 mm in from the inner edge of the lace ring.

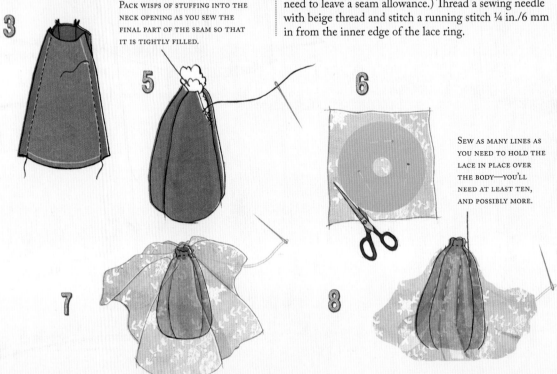

PACK WISPS OF STUFFING INTO THE NECK OPENING AS YOU SEW THE FINAL PART OF THE SEAM SO THAT IT IS TIGHTLY FILLED.

SEW AS MANY LINES AS YOU NEED TO HOLD THE LACE IN PLACE OVER THE BODY—YOU'LL NEED AT LEAST TEN, AND POSSIBLY MORE.

7 / Gather the inner edge of the lace slightly by pulling up the running stitch. Place the overskirt over the body, about ½ in./12 mm down from the top and gather the net more tightly, until it fits the circumference of the top of the body, then knot the beige thread. Arrange the gather evenly and hand sew the top of the skirt to the body.

8 / Use pins to fix the gathers neatly down the length of the body. Thread a sewing needle with a strand of metallic thread and stitch small lines in backstitch at even intervals from the top of the body to about halfway down, concealing them in the folds of the lace. You will need at least ten lines, and maybe more—check as you sew and stop when the overskirt is arranged neatly and the folds are held in place.

9 / Thread a needle with beige thread and sew a line of running stitches around the bottom edge of the lace overskirt, then pull the thread to gather the lace into a tight circle about ¾ in./2 cm in diameter at the base of the body. Use a small overstitch to sew the circle down to the center of the body base.

10 / Cut the thin brown leather into equal halves. Draw around the glove pattern piece on the right side of one half using a fabric pencil, then turn the pattern over and draw around it again on the same half. Thread the sewing machine with black thread and stitch a line down the center of both glove outlines. Then lay the second piece of leather under the first, right sides out, rethread the sewing machine with brown thread and stitch around both glove outlines through both thicknesses of leather, leaving the top end of both gloves open.

11 / Cut the gloves out as close to the stitching as possible without cutting it. Sew two tiny metallic glass beads along the black line of stitching on both gloves.

12 / Bend a pipe cleaner in half and push it inside one of the gloves, right to the end. Push a little soft toy stuffing around the pipe cleaner. Repeat with second glove.

13 / Sew the top of each glove to the body, lining it up with the edge of the lace overskirt. Sew the ends of the pipe cleaners firmly to the top of the body, folding the sharp ends over.

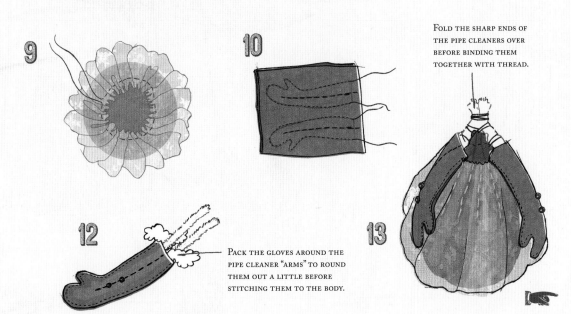

FOLD THE SHARP ENDS OF THE PIPE CLEANERS OVER BEFORE BINDING THEM TOGETHER WITH THREAD.

PACK THE GLOVES AROUND THE PIPE CLEANER "ARMS" TO ROUND THEM OUT A LITTLE BEFORE STITCHING THEM TO THE BODY.

TO MAKE THE BODICE AND SPEEDOMETER

14 / Distress the corduroy with candle wax, as shown on page 6, rubbing the waxed surface thoroughly. On the back side, use a fabric pencil to draw around the two bodice pieces (neck and chest)—keep the corduroy stripes running vertically and mark both A points. Cut both pieces out, leaving a ¼ in./6 mm seam allowance. With right sides together, pin the A points together, then pin along the whole seam, adjusting the curve with your fingers. Sew the seam with brown thread by machine or by hand using a backstitch. Trim the seam allowance to ⅛ in./3 mm, and open it out with your fingers.

15 / Thread the sewing machine with beige buttonhole thread on top and brown sewing thread on the bobbin. Sew a line of long stitches down the front of the bodice just right of the center. With the right sides together, sew the back seam of the bodice and trim the seam allowance to ⅛ in./3 mm.

16 / Turn the bodice right side out and rub with a scissor blade to smooth out the waxed surface. When it has regained its shape, fold the top and bottom seam allowances to the inside of the bodice. When they're creased at the right point, fold them out again, spread contact adhesive on the underside of the allowance, leave to dry for a minute or two, and turn them once again to the inside.

17 / Using brown thread, hand sew the small jump ring on the back seam of the bodice, ⅜ in./1 cm down from the top.

18 / Bind the plastic ring with three strands of antique gold embroidery floss, attaching one end to the ring with superglue, then winding along the ring. When the ring is covered, knot the end around it and glue in place.

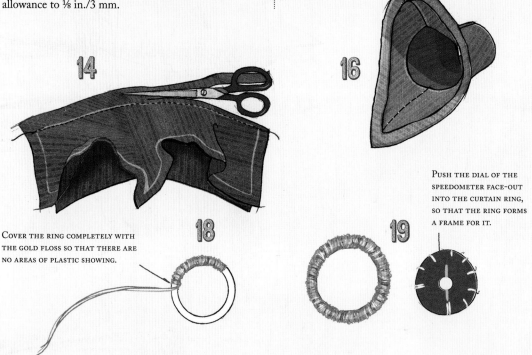

COVER THE RING COMPLETELY WITH THE GOLD FLOSS SO THAT THERE ARE NO AREAS OF PLASTIC SHOWING.

PUSH THE DIAL OF THE SPEEDOMETER FACE-OUT INTO THE CURTAIN RING, SO THAT THE RING FORMS A FRAME FOR IT.

19 / Draw around the speedometer pattern with a fabric pencil on a double thickness of black felt and cut it out. Push the bradawl through the center point to make a small hole. Thread a sewing needle with white thread and stitch the marks around the dial; use a single strand of green embroidery floss to stitch the hands. Push the felt, face side out, into the covered ring from the back and position it on the bodice, ½ in./12 mm up from the bottom point.

20 / Draw around the speedometer with a fabric pencil on the bodice to mark its place, then remove it. Spread a thin layer of contact adhesive on the circle on the bodice front and on the back of the speedometer. While you wait a minute or two for it to dry, push a brown brad through the center hole in the speedometer and open the back, then press the completed speedometer in place on the front of the bodice.

21 / Place the bodice over the top of the body and pin it in position, one pin on the front point and two holding it about ½ in./12 mm behind each arm. Thread a needle with brown thread and sew it firmly at these three points. Pack the bodice with toy stuffing through the open neck.

TO MAKE THE HEAD

22 / Cut three squares from the piece of pink cotton, each measuring 3 in./7.5 cm square. Stack the squares and draw around the face pattern on the top layer, making sure that the pattern is placed on the bias. Sew around the curve of the face through all three layers with pink thread, leaving the top edge open.

23 / Trace around the cardstock face template on a piece of medium-weight cardstock and cut the face piece out. Slide it between the second and third layers of the cotton, then use toy stuffing to pad the face lightly between the first and second layer of cotton. Sew the top closed, and cut the face out, leaving a ¼ in./6 mm seam allowance all round it.

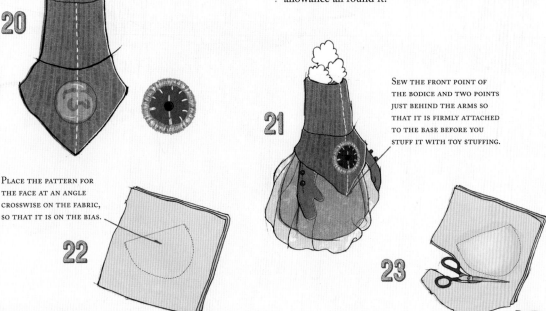

SEW THE FRONT POINT OF THE BODICE AND TWO POINTS JUST BEHIND THE ARMS SO THAT IT IS FIRMLY ATTACHED TO THE BASE BEFORE YOU STUFF IT WITH TOY STUFFING.

PLACE THE PATTERN FOR THE FACE AT AN ANGLE CROSSWISE ON THE FABRIC, SO THAT IT IS ON THE BIAS.

24 / Lay the pattern piece for the hair over the sewn face and use a pencil to draw the inner shape of the hair onto the face.

25 / Fold the pink knit fabric in half lengthwise and cut it into two rectangles, each measuring 6 x 4 in./ 15 x 10 cm. With right sides together, draw around the hair pattern piece with a fabric pencil on the top piece of fabric. Sew around the outer line, leaving the neck open. Cut the hair out, leaving a ⅛ in./3 mm seam allowance, with ¼ in./6 mm at the neck edge. Cut the face shape out from the top layer of fabric only, also leaving a ⅛ in./3 mm seam allowance. Turn the hair the right side out through the face hole.

26 / Starting with the narrowest tip, stuff the hair shape with soft toy stuffing so that it is full but not too tightly packed, then slip the face into position inside the hair pocket.

27 / Using pink thread, sew the hair around the face along the pencil line, using a small overstitch and turning in the seam allowance as you go. If the head and hair need extra padding, add a little through the neck. Stitch a small running stitch around the bottom edge of the neck and pull it tight.

28 / Use the fine, deep-pink permanent marker to draw on the lips and nose, using the photograph of the complete figure for reference.

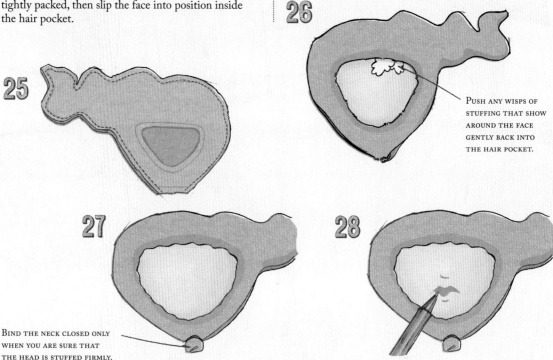

PUSH ANY WISPS OF STUFFING THAT SHOW AROUND THE FACE GENTLY BACK INTO THE HAIR POCKET.

BIND THE NECK CLOSED ONLY WHEN YOU ARE SURE THAT THE HEAD IS STUFFED FIRMLY.

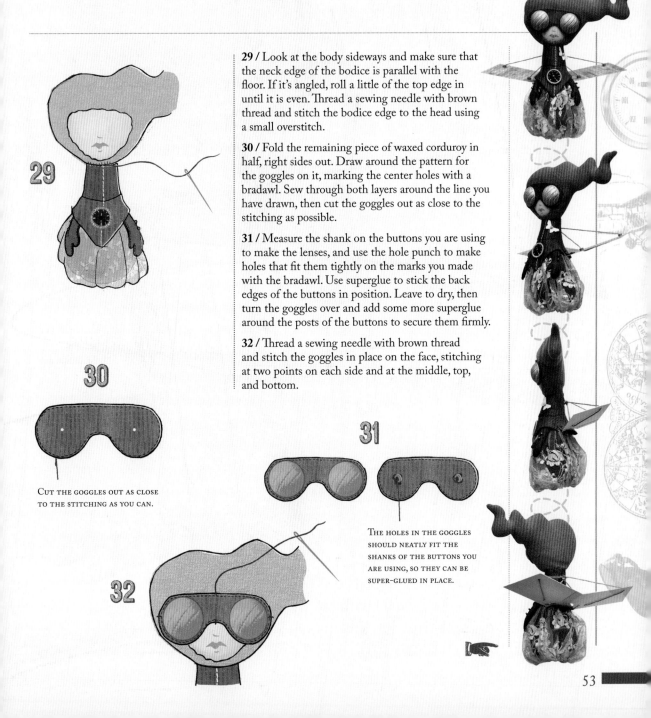

29 / Look at the body sideways and make sure that the neck edge of the bodice is parallel with the floor. If it's angled, roll a little of the top edge in until it is even. Thread a sewing needle with brown thread and stitch the bodice edge to the head using a small overstitch.

30 / Fold the remaining piece of waxed corduroy in half, right sides out. Draw around the pattern for the goggles on it, marking the center holes with a bradawl. Sew through both layers around the line you have drawn, then cut the goggles out as close to the stitching as possible.

31 / Measure the shank on the buttons you are using to make the lenses, and use the hole punch to make holes that fit them tightly on the marks you made with the bradawl. Use superglue to stick the back edges of the buttons in position. Leave to dry, then turn the goggles over and add some more superglue around the posts of the buttons to secure them firmly.

32 / Thread a sewing needle with brown thread and stitch the goggles in place on the face, stitching at two points on each side and at the middle, top, and bottom.

CUT THE GOGGLES OUT AS CLOSE
TO THE STITCHING AS YOU CAN.

THE HOLES IN THE GOGGLES
SHOULD NEATLY FIT THE
SHANKS OF THE BUTTONS YOU
ARE USING, SO THEY CAN BE
SUPER-GLUED IN PLACE.

TO MAKE THE WINGS

33 / Arrange the wing pattern piece on the heavy printed cardstock, keeping any pattern on the card parallel with the outside edge marked "O." Draw around the pattern piece in pencil and cut it out, then turn the pattern piece over, draw around it again and cut the second wing out. Finally, draw around the wing link piece on the cardstock and cut it out. Use a tiny quantity of superglue to stick the link to the underside of the two wings, leaving a slight gap between them at the join.

34 / Lay the wing pattern on top of the wings in turn and mark the four dots on them using a bradawl to pierce them. Widen the holes slightly and glue the brass tubular beads over each of them with superglue, being careful not to block the holes with glue.

35 / Draw around the wing fixing pattern piece twice on a leftover scrap of waxed corduroy. Mark the dots through the pattern piece with the bradawl and widen them a little to create small holes. Cut the pieces out without a seam allowance. Attach the fixings to the top sides of the wings by pushing a black brad through the holes in the wing fixings, then through the wings at points marked B, and opening each brad on the underside of the wing.

36 / Attach the wings in position by pushing two glass-headed pins through the empty holes on the wing fixings, and then through the bodice and into the sides of the body. The U shape of the wings should almost line up with the back bodice shape when you look down on the figure from above.

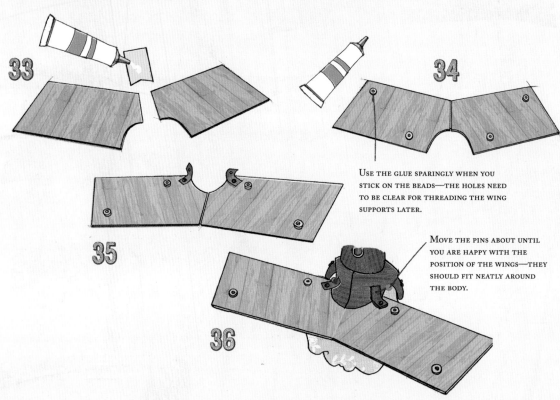

USE THE GLUE SPARINGLY WHEN YOU STICK ON THE BEADS—THE HOLES NEED TO BE CLEAR FOR THREADING THE WING SUPPORTS LATER.

MOVE THE PINS ABOUT UNTIL YOU ARE HAPPY WITH THE POSITION OF THE WINGS—THEY SHOULD FIT NEATLY AROUND THE BODY.

37

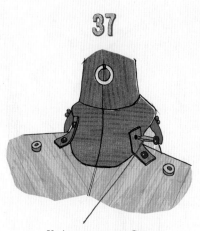

YOU'LL HAVE TO TURN CHARITY UPSIDE DOWN TO OPEN THE WING SUPPORT BRADS ON THE INSIDE OF THE BODICE.

37 / When you are happy with the placement, use the bradawl to enlarge the pinholes in the bodice and replace the holding pins with black brads. Hold the figure upside down and carefully open the brads on the inner edge of the bodice.

38 / Fold a 20 in./50 cm length of multi-strand green embroidery floss in half and thread the fold through the jump ring on the back. Pass the ends through the thread loop and pull tightly so the floss is secured on the ring. Pass one end down through the closest bead on the right wing and then up through the bead on the outside edge of the wing.

39 / Repeat with the other end of the thread and the left wing. Thread both ends back through the ring in the opposite directions, pull until you feel the wings are at the correct angle, and the thread is taut, then tie a knot and trim off any excess thread.

40 / Fold a tiny scrap of thick cream paper in half, place the butterfly pattern on the fold, draw around it, and cut out. Open out the butterfly shape and pin the "brooch" to Charity's neck using a small glass-headed pin, then dot with super glue to secure.

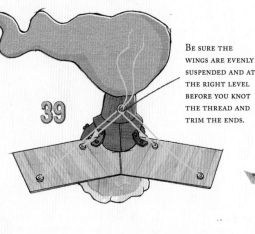

38

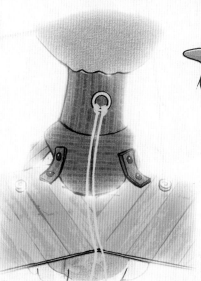

39

BE SURE THE WINGS ARE EVENLY SUSPENDED AND AT THE RIGHT LEVEL BEFORE YOU KNOT THE THREAD AND TRIM THE ENDS.

MINERVA DUPINE

MATERIALS & EQUIPMENT

- Houndstooth fabric for hat, 3 x 3 in./7.5 x 7.5 cm
- Scrap of thin brown leather, approximately 12 x 3 in./30 x 7.5 cm
- Herringbone wool suiting fabric, 18 x 3 in./ 46 x 7.5 cm
- Scrap of black felt, 3 x 2 in./7.5 x 5 cm
- Beige linen fabric, 7 x 8 in./17.5 x 20 cm
- Scrap of pink felt, 2 x 4 in./5 x 10 cm
- Black knit fabric (or you can use a piece of an old black sweater, felted by washing), 6 x 4 in./15 x 10 cm
- Black grosgrain ribbon, 3/8 in./9 mm diameter, 1 yd/1 m long
- Black grosgrain ribbon, 1/8 in./3 mm diameter, 1 yd/1 m long
- Sewing thread in red, black, beige, pink, and gray
- Buttonhole thread in black and pale brown
- Self-cover button with snap-on back, 1½ in./ 3.8 cm diameter
- Black 2-hole button, ½ in./13 mm diameter
- Assorted crafting brads in white, black, and brown, 1/8 in./3 mm diameter
- Cone-shaped silver bead, 12 mm long
- Glass-headed pin, approximately 1½ in./3.8 cm long
- Brass curtain ring, 1½ in./3.8 cm diameter
- Small clear plastic food container lid
- Jewelry chain, 3¼ in./8 cm long
- Gold jump ring, ½ in./13 mm diameter
- Small gold-colored jewelry hook clasp
- Small packet plastic toy-filling pellets
- Small quantity of soft toy stuffing
- Contact adhesive
- Superglue
- Latex adhesive
- Light fabric pencil
- Sharp scissors
- Sewing needle
- Dressmaking pins
- Hole punch
- Black fabric pen
- Needle-nosed pliers
- Bradawl

Note: Although it would be possible to make Minerva entirely by hand sewing, some parts are much easier to sew on a machine.

She may not belong to Pinkertons, but she's a complete professional in her field—and her field is detecting. She can unmask the fraudulent, track down stolen items—from husbands to jewelry—and she always gets her man (or woman). In her neat, practical dress, and wielding an immense magnifying glass with an outsize dose of savoir faire, Minerva Dupine is always in demand.

TINY CRAFT BRADS AND A LEATHER FRAME TURN A CURTAIN RING INTO AN IMPRESSIVE MAGNIFYING GLASS.

THE HAIR AND BANGS ARE MADE FROM STRETCHY KNIT FABRIC, SO EASE THE SEAMS INTO THE CURVES TO PUFF UP THE SHAPE.

THE STRIPES ON THE SKIRT AND BODICE ARE APPLIQUÉD STRIPS OF GROSGRAIN RIBBON.

MINERVA DUPINE STANDS 5 IN./ 13 CM TALL.

TO MAKE MINERVA DUPINE

1 / Photocopy, or scan and print, the pattern pieces from page 78 and cut them out.

TO MAKE THE HAT

2 / Ideally the hat should be made from a very small houndstooth, to match the scale of the figure. If you can't find a houndstooth, try a plain check or a wool fabric in a contrast color. Draw around the hat pattern on your fabric and cut it out. Cover the self-cover button as instructed on the packaging.

Tip: If you use a very thin fabric, cut a second circle of felt or another thicker fabric, align it with your first fabric circle, then cover the self-cover button with both layers to get a smooth result.

3 / Draw around the hat flap pattern piece twice on the thin brown leather and cut the two hat flaps out. Place them on opposite sides of the covered button and make tiny pencil marks on the covering to show the flap widths. Spread a thin layer of contact adhesive between the marks on the covered sides and the underside of the button, and another thin layer in a ⅜ in./1 cm-wide strip on the back of the hat flaps. Leave adhesive to dry for a few minutes.

4 / Stick the flaps to the sides of the button, folding in the wide ends and sticking them to its underside, along the rim. Tie the laces together in a bow for a full deerstalker effect, and use a tiny dot of superglue to secure the bow on top of the button.

TO MAKE THE BODY

5 / Mark out four skirt-panel pieces, the chest piece, and the body base piece on the herringbone fabric, drawing around the pattern pieces with a light fabric pencil on the wrong side of the material and leaving at least ¾ in./2 cm seam allowance around each pattern piece. Make sure that the stripes go straight up and down on each piece. Thread a sewing needle with red thread and sew a running stitch around the skirt panels and the chest piece, following the pencil outline, so that the pattern shapes are marked on the right side of the fabric.

EASE THE GLUED LEATHER GENTLY INTO THE SPACE BETWEEN THE BUTTON COVER AND ITS BACK.

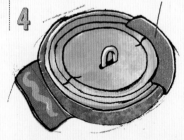

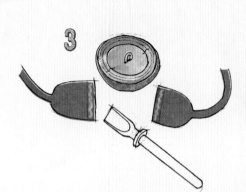

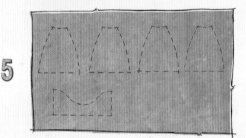

6 / Cut the wider grosgrain ribbon into twelve lengths, each 2¾ in./8 cm long. Each of the skirt panels will have three pieces sewn onto it. Arrange three pieces on the first skirt panel, as shown (The ribbon will extend above and below the skirt piece.), arranging the two outer pieces first, then the central one. Thread a needle with red thread and tack the ribbon in place, folding the upper part of the ribbons at an angle, as shown, then sew around each ribbon piece by machine with black thread. (If you prefer to hand sew, use a small backstitch.) Repeat with the other three skirt panels.

7 / Cut the narrow grosgrain ribbon into eleven lengths, each 2 in./5 cm long. Arrange the ribbons at even intervals vertically on the chest piece, each extending above and below the pattern edge, and machine or hand sew a single line of stitching down the center of each ribbon strip, using black thread.

8 / Cut out the chest and the four skirt panels, leaving a ⅜ in./1 cm seam allowance around each piece. Pull out the red running stitches marking out the pattern pieces.

9 / With the right sides together, sew the skirt panels together along their long edges by hand or machine, using black sewing thread. When you have stitched the four together in a row, trim the seam allowances down to ⅛ in./3 mm.

10 / Pin the long, straight side of the chest piece to the top of the stitched skirt and sew it in place, by hand or machine, using black sewing thread. Trim the seam allowance to ⅛ in./3 mm.

11 / Using black thread, sew the center back seam of the skirt and chest, making a cone shape, and trim the seam allowance to ⅛ in./3 mm.

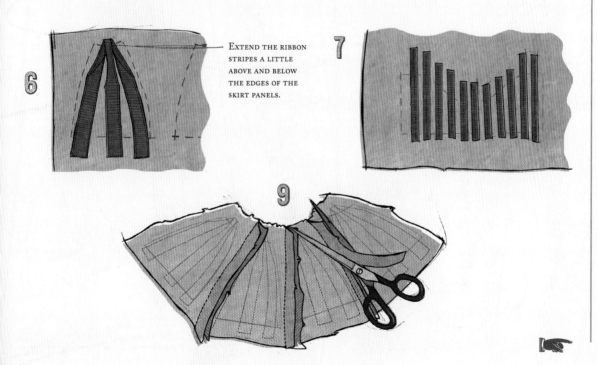

EXTEND THE RIBBON STRIPES A LITTLE ABOVE AND BELOW THE EDGES OF THE SKIRT PANELS.

12 / Cut the body base from the herringbone fabric, using a fabric pencil to mark the quarters as shown on the pattern, and leaving a ⅜ in./1 cm seam allowance. Pin the base piece into the open base of the skirt, right sides together, matching the seams on the skirt to the quarter marks on the base piece. Sew the base to the skirt using black thread. Trim the seam allowance to ⅛ in./3 mm. Turn the body right side out.

13 / Pour plastic toy-filling pellets into the body until it is quite tightly packed. Turn the seam allowance on the neck inwards and push a small amount of soft toy stuffing into the neck on top of the pellets.

14 / Cut the piece of black felt in half and spread one side of each piece with a thin layer of latex adhesive. Leave to dry for a few minutes, then press the glued sides together to stick. Cut the pattern piece for the body plug from the felt. Use a needle and black thread to stitch it onto the top of the body using a small overstitch.

TO MAKE THE HEAD AND HAIR

15 / Cut the beige linen in half and align the two pieces, one on top of the other. Place the pattern piece for the face on the top piece and draw around it with a fabric pencil. Sew the two pieces together with beige thread, leaving the top open, but extending your stitching line into the seam allowance. Cut the face out, leaving a ⅜ in./1 cm seam allowance at the top, but trimming around the stitched portion to ⅛ in./3 mm. Turn the face right side out and stuff it with soft toy stuffing.

16 / Cut the piece of pink felt in half, and spread a thin layer of latex adhesive on one side of each half. Leave to dry for a few minutes, then press the glued sides together to stick. Draw around the pattern piece for the top of the head and cut the circle out. Use the hole punch to cut a ³/₁₆ in./4 mm hole through the center of the circle.

TAP THE BODY DOWN ON A HARD SURFACE A FEW TIMES TO SETTLE THE PELLETS BEFORE ADDING THE LAST PIECES OF STUFFING IN THE BODICE.

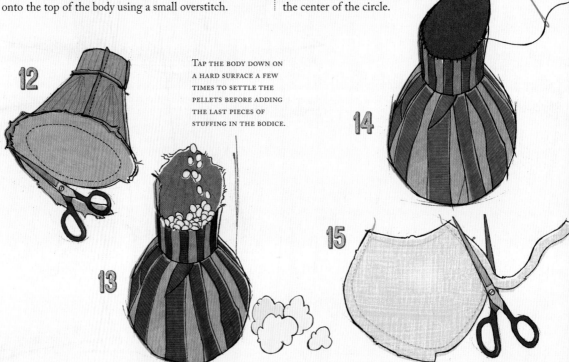

17 / Fold down the seam allowance on the top of the face and place the felt circle over it, lining up the marks shown on the pattern piece with the seams. Thread a needle with pink thread and stitch the circle in place using a small overstitch. Just before completing the circle, while there is still a small gap, push some more stuffing into the head to fill it as full as possible.

18 / Draw around the bangs pattern piece on the back of the black knit fabric with a light fabric pencil. The "knit" of the fabric should run vertically up and down the bangs piece, so that the piece will have the greatest amount of stretch from side to side. Cut the bangs out leaving a ¼ in./6 mm seam allowance.

19 / With right sides together, stitch the two straight edges of the bangs piece together with black sewing thread, and then turn it right side out.

20 / Pull the bangs over the top of the head, like a hat, with the seam at the back. Turn the seam allowance under around the edge of the face, checking the photograph so that you get the right balance of bangs to face. Pin the bangs in place.

21 / Make sure that you can see the hole in the pink felt head through the top of the bangs. Thread a needle with black buttonhole thread, double it, and knot the end. Push the needle through the back of the head and bring it out through the punched felt hole at the top of the head. Pass the needle through the loop on the back of the button/hat, then back through the punched felt hole, and back out at the back of the head. Pull the thread tight so that the hat sits flush to the top of the head, then knot it and trim. Add a tiny dot of superglue under the button at the front to hold the hat firmly in position.

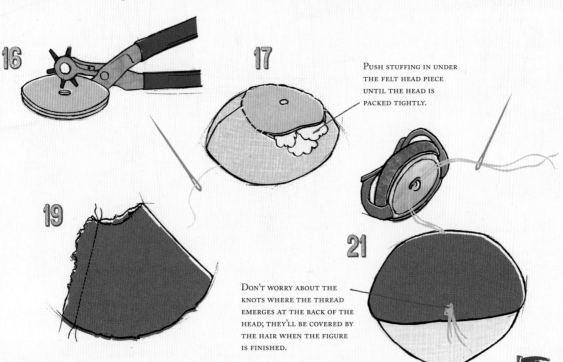

PUSH STUFFING IN UNDER THE FELT HEAD PIECE UNTIL THE HEAD IS PACKED TIGHTLY.

DON'T WORRY ABOUT THE KNOTS WHERE THE THREAD EMERGES AT THE BACK OF THE HEAD; THEY'LL BE COVERED BY THE HAIR WHEN THE FIGURE IS FINISHED.

22 / Thread a needle with black sewing thread, then sew on the black button for the right eye. Knot the thread. Place a ⅛ in./3 mm-diameter white brad through one of the holes in the button and open it out on the back of the button to secure. Draw on the right eyelashes and the left eye and lashes with a black fabric pen.

23 / Sew the cone-shaped silver bead in place on the side of the head using gray sewing thread. (Check the position with the photograph.)

24 / Fold a piece of the black knit fabric into a double rectangle, place the hair pattern on the top, and draw around it with a fabric pencil. Stitch around the pencil line with black thread, leaving the curve open between numbers 1 and 4, marked on the pattern piece.

25/ Cut the hair out, leaving a ⅛ in./3 mm seam allowance all round except for the open edge which should keep a ¼ in./6 mm seam allowance. Snip toward the stitching at the angles of the hair shape, being careful not to cut the stitches themselves, then turn it right side out. Pad the hair slightly with soft toy stuffing, then turn in the seam allowance of the opening and stitch it closed.

26 / Thread a needle with black thread and sew the head to the body using a small overstitch. Pin the hair to the back of the head at the four points marked on the pattern.

27/ Using a sewing needle threaded with black thread, catch the hair to the head at the point marked 1 on the original paper pattern, then make a long running stitch to catch the front of the hair and the bangs piece together, stitching toward point 2. This will pull the hair forward and join the bangs and hair together. Stitch toward point 3, using the same technique and catching the hair and bangs together under the back of the hat, and then down toward point 4. When you reach point 4, fasten off the thread.

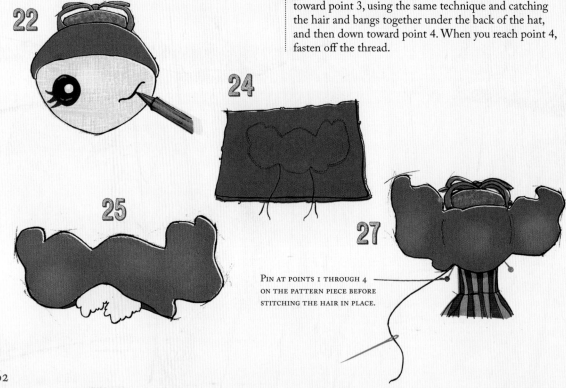

PIN AT POINTS 1 THROUGH 4
ON THE PATTERN PIECE BEFORE
STITCHING THE HAIR IN PLACE.

28 / Use pliers to bend the glass-headed pin at an angle of 90 degrees ⅜ in./1 cm from the sharp end. Use superglue to stick it into the hole in the conical bead on the side of the head to make an "antenna." Prop the figure so that the pin holds it until the glue has dried.

TO MAKE THE EYEGLASS

29 / Place the leather eye piece pattern on the back of one end of the strip of leather and draw around it with a fabric pencil. Mark the four holes for the brads with a bradawl through the pattern, remove the pattern, and use the bradawl to enlarge the holes a little. Cut the eye piece out along the marked outline, without a seam allowance.

30 / Choose four brads from the assorted packet (We used two brown and two beige.) and push them through the holes in the leather from the right side, opening them on the back of the leather.

31 / Wrap the four strips around the brass curtain ring from the outside into the center of the ring (the loop of the ring should have two arms on each side of it). Use tiny dots of superglue underneath the brads and stick them to the ring.

If the brads extend beyond the leather when their backs are opened, trim their "arms" a little.

Use the pliers to bend a right angle in the pin before inserting it into the bead.

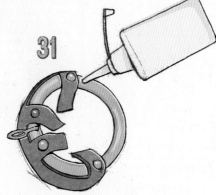

32 / Spread a thin layer of latex adhesive on the ends of the strips, on the wrong side, and another on the inside of the curved leather piece just outside the ring. Leave to dry for a few minutes then press together to stick.

33 / Draw around the lens piece pattern on the plastic lid and cut it out. Place a very thin line of super glue around its edge and stick it onto the back of the curtain ring. The horizontal mark should be horizontal in the eyepiece.

34 / Cut a tiny strip from the leather, measuring 2¼ x ⅜ in./7 x 1 cm, spread the back with a thin layer of latex adhesive, and leave it to dry. Thread one end of the length of chain onto the gold jump ring, and slip the leather strip through the ring and fold it in half to make the fob.

35 / Pierce two holes in the leather with the bradawl and place two brads through them, opening the brads on the other side—you may need to trim them a little.

36 / Attach the small hook clasp to the other end of the chain, and clip it onto the loop on the side of the curtain ring.

37 / Mark the outline of the curved leather edge of the eye piece on the head, either with pins or tiny marks made with a fabric pencil. Spread a thin layer of latex adhesive where the eye piece will go. Glue an area about ⅜ in./1 cm wide along the inside edge of the leather piece. Leave the glue to dry for a few minutes, then stick the eye piece in place on the face. Place the fob on the skirt so that the chain hangs down below it in a loop, but still clears the ground. (Check with the photograph of the finished figure if you're not sure.)

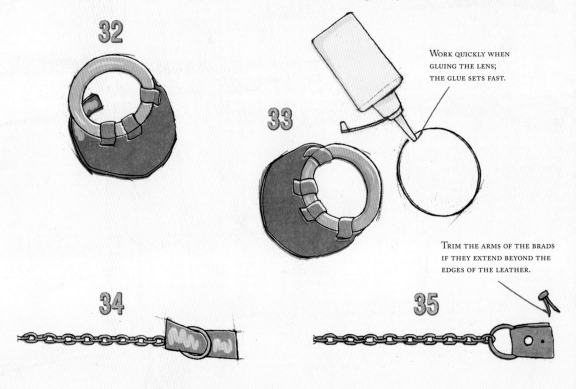

WORK QUICKLY WHEN
GLUING THE LENS;
THE GLUE SETS FAST.

TRIM THE ARMS OF THE BRADS
IF THEY EXTEND BEYOND THE
EDGES OF THE LEATHER.

37

MARK THE PLACEMENT OF THE
EYE PIECE AND FOB CAREFULLY
BEFORE APPLYING THE GLUE.

TO MAKE THE BOW

38 / Cut a rectangle measuring 6¾ x 2¼ in./17 x 5.5 cm from the remains of the brown leather. On the back, draw two lines, parallel with the long edges and ¾ in./2 cm in from the edge. Spread a thin layer of latex adhesive down each edge to the line and leave to dry for a few minutes, then turn the edges over to the line and press down to stick. Glue into a loop by overlapping the ends.

39 / Thread a needle with pale brown buttonhole thread and make a line of stitches across the hoop where the ends overlap. Fasten off the thread. Flatten the hoop with the stitching to one side. Measure to find the middle of the strip and bind some buttonhole thread around it to make the bow shape.

40 / Cut a small strip of leather measuring 2 x ¾ in./ 5 x 2 cm and superglue the middle of the bow around the binding. Make sure that the overlap of the strip is on the same side of the bow as the stitching. Use contact adhesive to stick the bow onto the back, just below the waistline.

38

39

40

FERRIS SCAPULA

MATERIALS & EQUIPMENT

- Beige linen, approximately 8 x 4 in./20 x 10 cm
- Dark brown woolen fabric, 9 x 4½ in./23 x 11.5 cm
- Small scrap of thin gauze, about 3 x 2 in./7.5 x 5 cm
- White felt, 2 x 2 in./5 x 5 cm
- Black felt, 1 x 1½ in., plus strip ⅛ x 3¾ in./ 3 mm x 9.5 cm for tie; 6 x 6 in./15 x 15 cm for hat
- Small scrap of brown leather, about ⅛ x 3 in./ 3 mm x 7.5 cm
- Buttonhole thread in white and beige
- Sewing thread in brown, beige, and black
- Gold plastic bottle top, about 1 in./2.5 cm diameter
- Fine gold leather necklace cord, 18 in./45 cm long
- 4 small "coil clasp" jewelry findings, about ⅜ in./1 cm long
- 2 slightly mismatched round black beads, about 3 mm diameter
- 1 tiny metallic bead
- Small scrap of brown paper
- Small corked glass bottle, approx 1¼ in./3 cm high
- 4 jump rings, ¼ in./6 mm diameter
- Pair inexpensive tweezers
- Small quantity of soft toy stuffing
- Contact adhesive
- Latex adhesive
- Glue stick
- Superglue
- Epoxy glue
- Light and dark fabric pencils
- Brown and gray drawing chalks
- Sharp scissors
- Sewing and beading needles
- Craft knife
- Bradawl

Note: You can make Ferris Scapula entirely by hand sewing, but some parts are easier to sew on a machine.

Travel-stained and weary, Ferris Scapula carries the tools of his medical trade wherever he goes. There's an outsized pair of tweezers on his back and an ominously labeled bottle in his hand; his top hat looks rusty with wear, but his mask guarantees that he, at least, is protected from infection. Where he practices (and on whom) remains a mystery, but be thankful that you're not the patient at the sharp end of his scalpel.

THE TOP HAT IS ARTIFICIALLY AGED TO GIVE IT A BATTERED, DISTRESSED APPEARANCE.

FOLLOW THE PATTERN CAREFULLY TO PIERCE THE HOLES IN THE FACE MASK EVENLY.

THE BEAD EYES ARE SEWN DEEPLY INTO THE FACE TO CREATE SLIGHTLY SUNKEN SOCKETS.

FERRIS SCAPULA STANDS 6 IN./ 15 CM TALL.

FILL THE BOTTLE WITH CINNAMON, SAND, OR ANY OTHER POWDER ACCORDING TO PREFERENCE. BAKING SODA WILL LOOK LIKE ARSENIC!

TO MAKE FERRIS SCAPULA

1 / Photocopy, or scan and print, the pattern pieces from page 79 and cut them out. Cut the short vertical slits in the head piece; these will enable you to mark the stitched brow lines on Ferris's face.

TO MAKE THE HEAD

2 / Cut the beige linen in half so that you have two squares. Draw around the head pattern on one square with a fabric pencil, then fold down the brow on the pattern to the full length of the slits and mark the brow lines with a fabric pencil.

3 / Thread the machine with white buttonhole thread and sew along the brow lines on the front head piece. (If you don't want to machine sew, you can sew by hand using a small backstitch.)

4 / Sandwich the two face squares together, leaving the pencil outline on the front head piece facing outwards. Stitch along the pencil outline, leaving the neck open between the marks.

5 / Cut the head out, leaving a ¼ in./6 mm seam allowance. Turn it right side out, then pad the head with soft toy stuffing through the open neck.

TO MAKE THE BODY

6 / Cut the strip of brown wool fabric into two squares. Align the squares, place the body pattern on the top square, and draw around it with a fabric pencil.

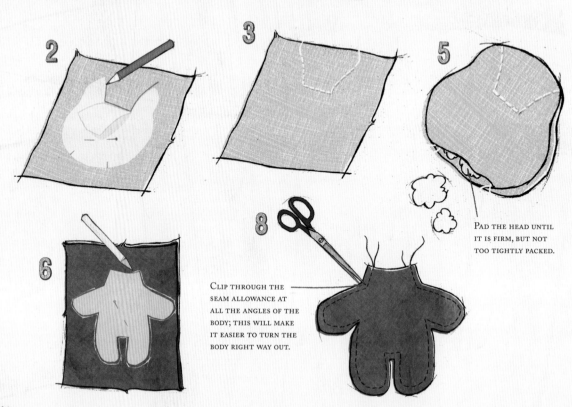

PAD THE HEAD UNTIL IT IS FIRM, BUT NOT TOO TIGHTLY PACKED.

CLIP THROUGH THE SEAM ALLOWANCE AT ALL THE ANGLES OF THE BODY; THIS WILL MAKE IT EASIER TO TURN THE BODY RIGHT WAY OUT.

7 / Thread the machine with brown sewing thread and sew the two layers together, using a small stitch, following the pencil line and leaving the neck open between the pattern marks.

8 / Cut out the body, leaving a ⅛ in./3 mm seam allowance. Cut tiny snips through the seam allowance toward the stitching, taking care not to cut into the stitching itself.

9 / Turn the body right side out. Use the points of the scissors or tweezers to push wisps of stuffing down into the legs, then, when they are lightly padded, hand or machine sew a line across the top of each with beige buttonhole thread.

10 / Stuff the arms in the same way as the legs and use beige buttonhole thread to sew a line across the end of each where it joins the body.

11 / Stuff the body and neck and turn the seam allowance at the top of the neck inward. Push the neck of the head into the open neck of the body and use beige sewing thread to sew the head onto the body with a small overstitch.

TO MAKE THE MASK

12 / Cut the depth of the bottle top down to ¼ in./6 mm, using a craft knife or sharp scissors.

13 / Use a bradawl to mark the ventilation holes from the mask pattern onto the top of the lid and pierce through the plastic with the bradawl to make a pattern of neat holes. Pierce four holes for the mask straps into the sides of the mask, two on each side (at 2, 4, 8, and 10 o'clock), using the bradawl. If there are any rough burrs of plastic left, trim them off with a craft knife.

KEEP THE STITCHES JOINING THE HEAD TO THE BODY AS SMALL AND UNNOTICEABLE AS POSSIBLE.

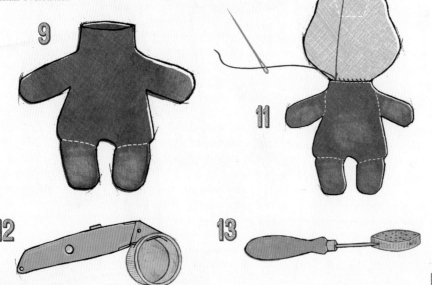

14 / Cut the gold necklace cord into two equal lengths. Thread the cord across the back of the mask, through the side holes, one length at the top and the other at the bottom.

15 / Cut two circles from the gauze, using the fabric for mask pattern, and align them. Shred the edges slightly with your fingers or the points of sharp scissors.

16 / Sew the mask fabric onto the head by hand, using beige sewing thread and following the stitching line of the circle marked on the pattern. Take small, single stitches, making sure to catch the linen of the head fabric through the bandage.

17 / Use the same thread to sew the mask on top of the fabric, using the holes that the necklace cords pass through.

18 / Thread the four coil clasps, one onto each strap, and knot the straps securely at the back of the head.

19 / Sew the two black bead eyes on the face using black sewing thread. Pass the thread right through the head and take a tiny stitch at the back as you sew—this will create a slight pucker or "eye socket" at the front of the face.

TO MAKE THE BIB

20 / Cut the bib from white felt using the bib pattern. For the tie, cut the main shape from black felt and also cut a thin strip of black felt ⅛ in./3 mm wide and 3¾ in./9.5 cm long. Use contact adhesive to stick the center portion of the strip along the top line of the bib, even with the bottom of the slot—spread a thin layer of adhesive on both surfaces, leave to dry for a few minutes, then press together.

21 / Glue the top of the tie to the back of the bib with contact adhesive. Turn the rest of the tie to the front of the bib. Use black sewing thread and a beading needle to stitch it in place, using the tiny metallic bead as a tie pin.

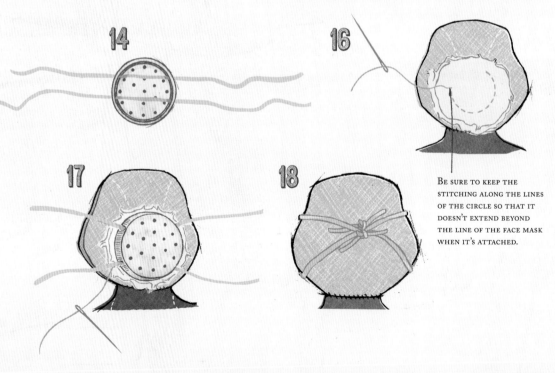

BE SURE TO KEEP THE STITCHING ALONG THE LINES OF THE CIRCLE SO THAT IT DOESN'T EXTEND BEYOND THE LINE OF THE FACE MASK WHEN IT'S ATTACHED.

22 / Use latex adhesive to stick the bib in place on the front of the body, and to stick the tie ends around the neck, overlapping them at the back.

TO MAKE THE HAT AND ACCESSORIES

23 / Cut the black felt into two rectangles of equal size and use contact adhesive to stick them together. Cut the hat, hat top, and hat brim from the double layered felt, using the patterns.

24 / To make the hat's body, roll the piece into a tube, butt the edges together, and hand sew along the seam using black thread. Align the hat top circle with the top of the cylinder and sew it in place with a small overstitch.

25 / Run a thin line of contact adhesive along the bottom edge of the hat tube and along the inner edge of the brim piece. Allow to dry for a few minutes, then press the glued brim along the wavy edge of the tube, matching the A points marked on the pattern pieces.

GENTLY MANIPULATE THE HAT BRIM TO FIT ALONG THE WAVY BASE OF THE HAT CROWN—THE CURVED LINE HELPS TO GIVE THE HAT ITS AGED APPEARANCE.

26 / Draw a tiny skull and crossbones on a scrap of brown paper and stick it to the glass bottle with the glue stick. Fill the bottle with whatever you like; the one in the photograph is full of sand. Attach the bottle to the left arm by winding brown thread around its neck, then stitching and knotting it through the left arm.

27 / Join the four jump rings together, feed the end ring over the open pincers of the tweezers and use superglue to stick it in place.

28 / Fold one end of the thin strip of brown leather over the jump ring farthest away from the tweezers, and stick it down with epoxy glue. Sling the leather across Ferris Scapula's front, so that the tweezers are slung across his back, and use superglue to stick the other end of the leather strip around the top end of the tweezers. Leave to dry.

29 / To give Ferris a well-traveled appearance, rub a little chalk dust from the gray and brown drawing chalks onto the tips of your fingers and rub it onto his clothes and face, "dirtying" them a little. Work slowly and keep the end result subtle.

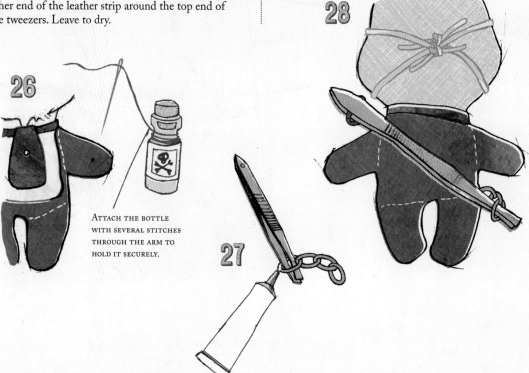

ATTACH THE BOTTLE WITH SEVERAL STITCHES THROUGH THE ARM TO HOLD IT SECURELY.

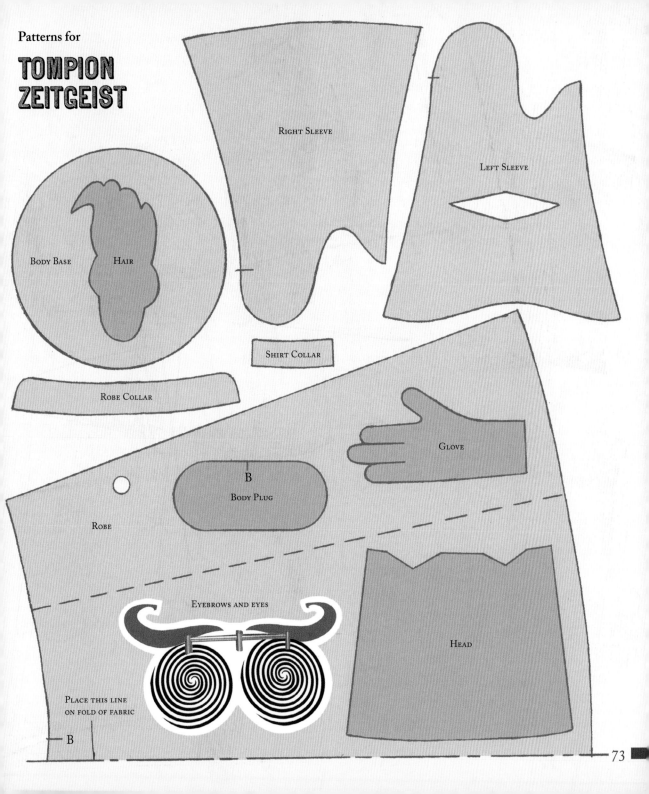

Patterns for

TOMPION ZEITGEIST

RIGHT SLEEVE

LEFT SLEEVE

BODY BASE   HAIR

SHIRT COLLAR

ROBE COLLAR

GLOVE

B
BODY PLUG

ROBE

EYEBROWS AND EYES

HEAD

PLACE THIS LINE
ON FOLD OF FABRIC

B

73

Patterns for

FATHOMLESS TILT

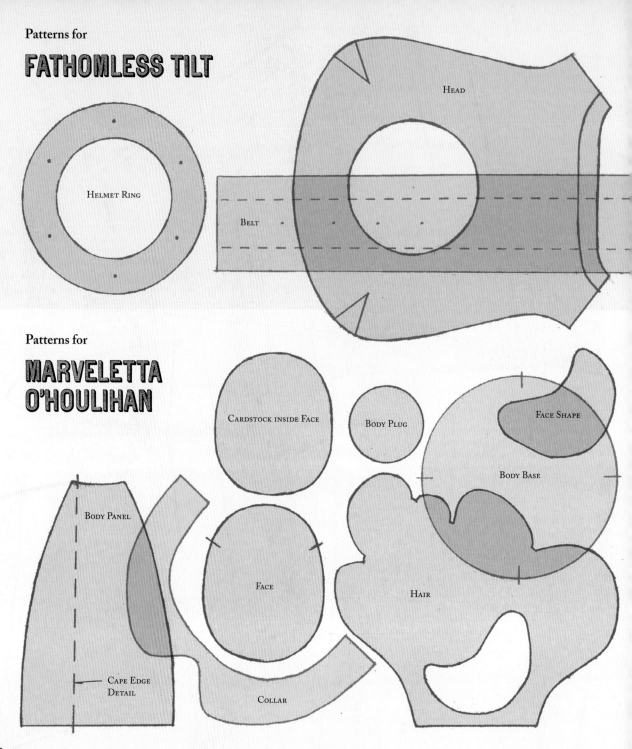

HELMET RING

HEAD

BELT

Patterns for

MARVELETTA
O'HOULIHAN

CARDSTOCK INSIDE FACE

BODY PLUG

FACE SHAPE

BODY BASE

BODY PANEL

FACE

HAIR

CAPE EDGE
DETAIL

COLLAR

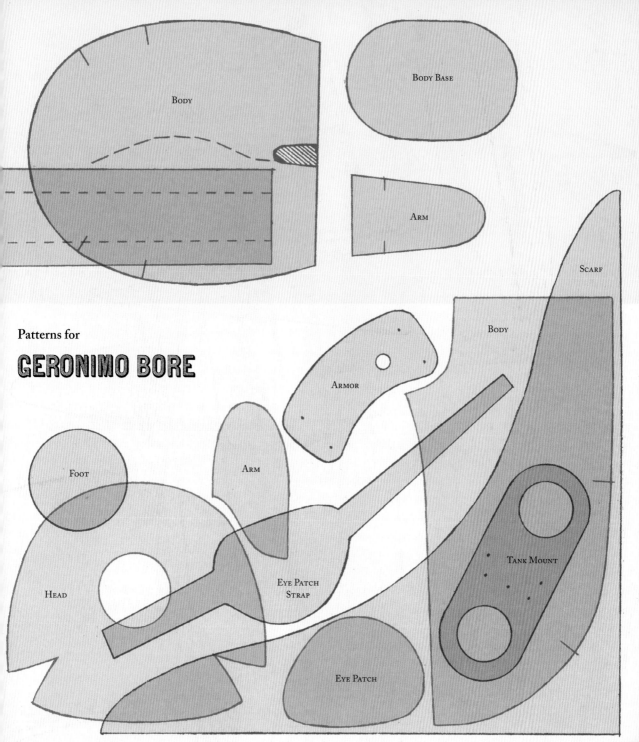

BODY

BODY BASE

ARM

SCARF

Patterns for

GERONIMO BORE

ARMOR

BODY

FOOT

ARM

HEAD

EYE PATCH
STRAP

TANK MOUNT

EYE PATCH

Patterns for
FLOYD FASTKNIGHT

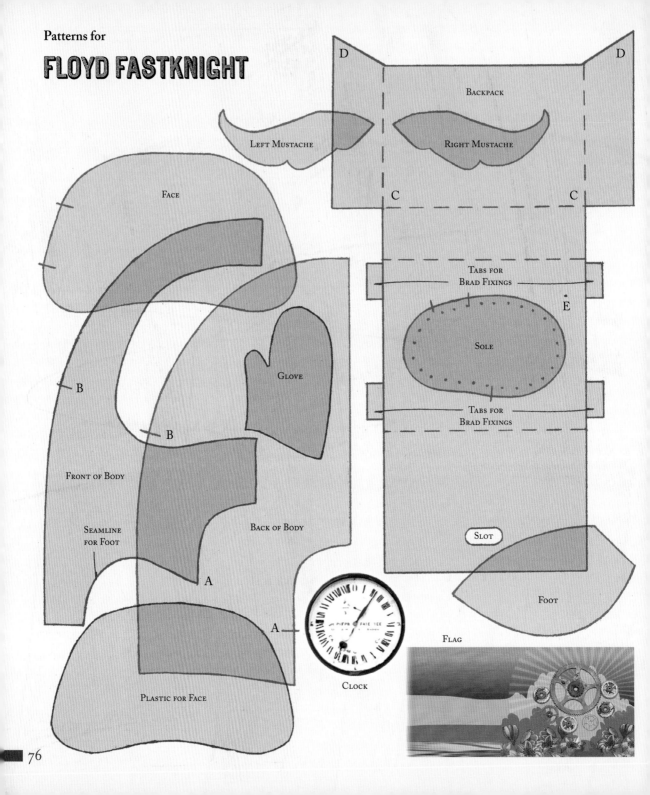

D   D

Backpack

Left Mustache

Right Mustache

C   C

Face

Tabs for
Brad Fixings

E

Sole

Glove

B

Tabs for
Brad Fixings

B

Front of Body

Back of Body

Seamline
for Foot

Slot

A

A

Foot

Flag

Clock

Plastic for Face

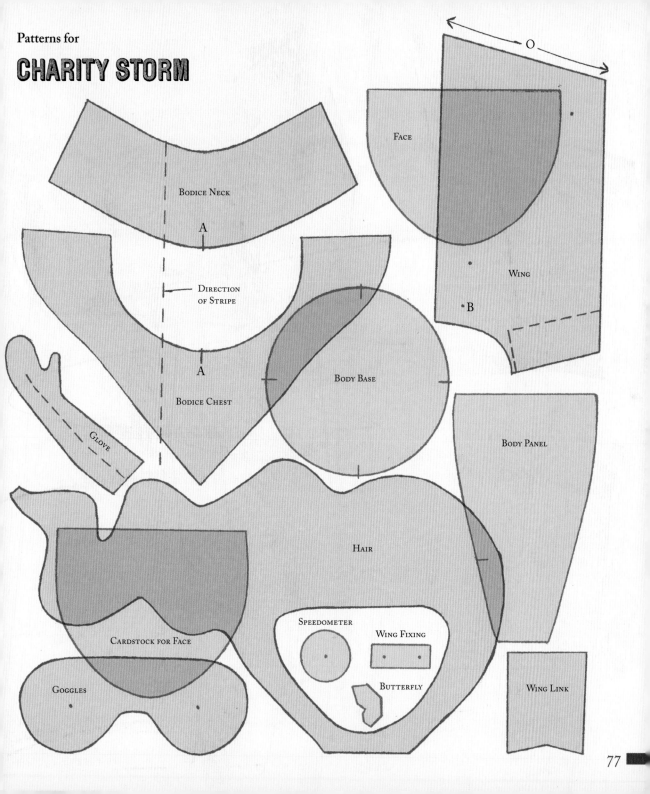

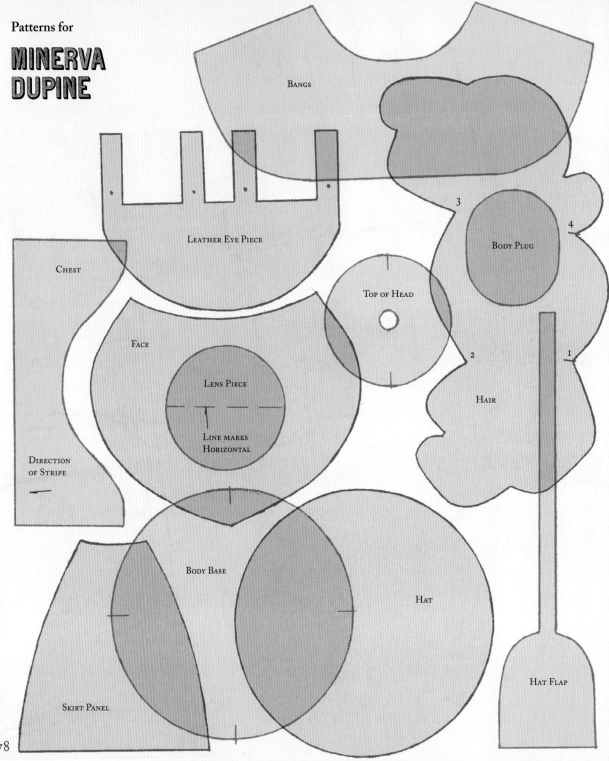

Patterns for

MINERVA DUPINE

Bangs

3

4

Body Plug

Leather Eye Piece

Chest

Top of Head

2

1

Face

Hair

Lens Piece

Line marks
Horizontal

Direction
of Stripe

Body Base

Hat

Skirt Panel

Hat Flap

Patterns for

FERRIS SCAPULA

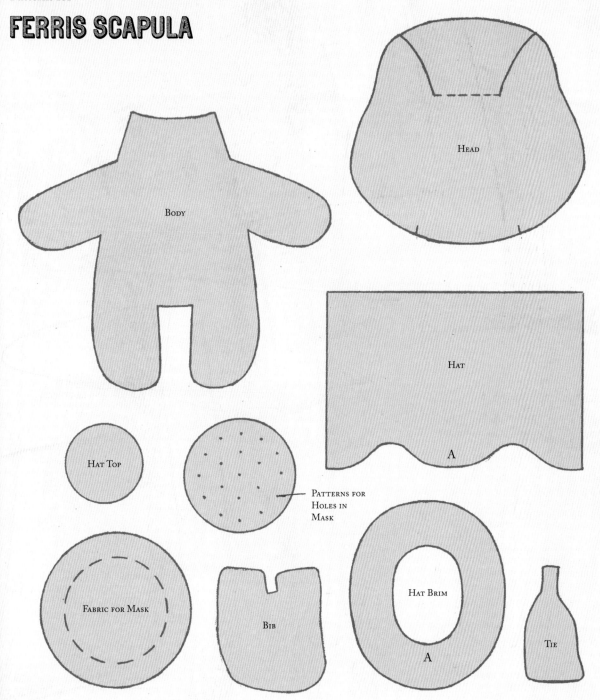

Head

Body

Hat

A

Hat Top

Patterns for
Holes in
Mask

Fabric for Mask

Bib

Hat Brim

A

Tie

INDEX